"Back to First Principles"

George Washington, by Charles Willson Peale, 1795

"Back to First Principles"

A Conversation with George Washington

Jay A. Parry

Author of *The Real George Washington*

STONEWELL PRESS

ISBN 978-1-62730-096-4

Published by Stonewell Press, Salt Lake City, Utah.
Printed in the United States of America.

Stonewell Press and the Stonewell Press logo are trademarks of Stonewell Press.

www.stonewellpress.com
editor@stonewellpress.com

Contents

George Washington, by Gilbert Stuart, begun 1795

Introduction

The events that brought me face to face with a gracious and dignified George Washington are too incredible—and too complicated—to recount here. Suffice it to say that it happened, and I was both moved and deeply humbled at the opportunity. I had been an admirer of his for many decades and, more recently, had become a careful student of his life and words.

He was an imposing figure. He stood at about six feet two or three inches. He was muscular and massive in frame; he may have weighed some 220 pounds. His hands were huge, perhaps larger than I have ever seen on a man. I'm not sure what I expected in terms of clothing—perhaps a military uniform or a formal suit of clothing such as a gentleman would wear on special occasions. Instead he was dressed in the simple, plain, well-cared-for clothing of a farmer who actually goes out into the field. He said at one point that the place he loved more than any other in the world—more than the halls of Congress or the ruling seat of government—was the quiet fields of his farm, Mount Vernon.

His sense of humor was surprising. His candor was refreshing. His vocabulary and facility of expression were amazing. The depth of his philosophy was impressive. People don't think and talk like that anymore, I thought, in these days of the quick sound bite and the hasty solution—these days when most popular publications are written for an eighth-grade reader or less. It was clear how very much he loved the principles of freedom and the land of America. But he was deeply troubled by the way in which the country he had helped to establish through, as he put it, the sacrifice of much "blood and treasure," had deteriorated both morally and in terms of sound principles of constitutional government.

It also was inspiring to see how his speeches and letters, all written more than two centuries ago, resonated so clearly for our day. It's true that his writing style is much more formal than we commonly use today. From our point of view, it might sometimes feel a little stiff or stilted. But, just as with the Bible or Shakespeare, it was always appropriate for its time. A little familiarity only endears the style to us, and soon we are anxious to read more. (To facilitate the reading of this account, however, some spelling, capitalization, and punctuation has been changed to fit with modern conventions.)

Suppose you had a chance to interview George Washington, to try to get to know him a little better, to ask him how he feels about the direction in which America is going, to learn directly from the words of the Father of Our Country. What would he tell you? Luckily, his words have been carefully recorded and preserved. One of the most complete collections of his writings is *The Writings of George Washington,* edited by John C. Fitzpatrick; it runs thirty-seven large and impressive volumes. Most sources in the following interview cite the Fitzpatrick collection, using the abbreviation "F," followed by the volume number, page number, and the date. Even more comprehensive is the sixty-three-volume *The Papers of George Washington,* which includes not only correspondence he wrote but also letters he received. (A bibliographical listing of that and other sources is found at the end of the book.)

In this opportunity to meet with President Washington, I was able to ask many questions of current concern. His answers, pulled verbatim from his writings, elucidate principles and underscore vital truth that can give us essential guidance today. Occasionally, the reader will see phrases or sentences at the beginning of a Washington statement that are not in quotation marks. Such are *not* pulled from Washington's writings but were inserted by the compiler of this work to help provide transitions where needed. I have also included a number of other transitional interchanges to establish a flow of conversation; they also can be identified by the absence of quotation marks.

Washington at Home, by Alonzo Cappel, 1867

A Little Background

Jay Parry: President Washington, it truly is a singular privilege to finally meet you. I've admired you for decades. Your wisdom and common sense are legendary. Of course, your experience as one of our founding fathers puts you in a class all by yourself—farmer and philosopher, a member of the Continental Congress, commander in chief during the Revolutionary War, president of the Constitutional Convention, first president of the United States. But before we talk about those things from a political point of view, we'd like to get to know you a little better personally. Besides what I've mentioned, what should we most know about you?

George Washington: I was married to Martha Custis. I called her Patsy as a special term of endearment. We had a remarkable life together, raising her children and grandchildren, dealing with extraordinary challenges, trying to build America.

JP: Was she the love of your life?

GW: When I was serving in the Continental Congress, war with Great Britain was brewing. Because of my military background during the French and Indian War, the members of Congress seemed to feel that I was a natural choice to lead the American efforts against the British, and they drafted me for that position. Here's what I wrote to my beloved Patsy: "You may believe me, my dear Patsy, when I assure you . . . that, so far from seeking this appointment, I have used every endeavor in my power to avoid it, not only from my unwillingness to part with you and the family, but from a consciousness of its being a trust too great for my capacity." Then I added my deepest feelings: "I should enjoy more real happiness in one month with you at home, than I have the most distant prospect of finding abroad, if my stay were to be seven times seven years. . . . I shall feel no pain from the toil or the danger of the campaign; my unhappiness will flow from the uneasiness I know you will feel from being left alone."[1]

JP: You loved being with her—and you loved being on your farm.

GW: Yes. I was at war for about seven years. I was gone for months at a time to meetings of Congress and to the Constitutional Convention. I was gone for most of eight years when I served as president. And although I was fully willing to serve, I repeatedly expressed my simple desire to go home. For example, in 1782, while I was still serving as commander in chief, I indicated to Archibald Cary, one of my fellow Virginians, "I can truly say that the first wish of my soul is to return speedily into the bosom of that country which gave me birth, and, in the sweet enjoyment of domestic happiness and the company of a few friends, to end my days in quiet."[2]

JP: Did that day come at the end of the war?

GW: I certainly was confident it would. In 1783, "I anticipate[d]with pleasure the day, and that I trust not far off, when I [should] quit the busy scenes of a military employment and retire to the more tranquil walks of domestic life." I left my "domestic retirement" at Mount Vernon "with the greatest reluctance" and had "never ceased to sigh" for it "through a long and painful ab-

---

1. F 3:293; 1775.
2. F 24:348; 1782.

sence." When I retired, I expected to be "remote from the noise and trouble of the world," where "I meditate to pass the remainder of life in a state of undisturbed repose."[1]

When that day finally came, I said, "The scene is at last closed. I feel myself eased of a load of public care. I hope to spend the remainder of my days in cultivating the affections of good men, and in the practice of the domestic virtues."[2]

JP: It sounds like you finally attained your desire.

GW: At first I was perfectly satisfied. I noted that "at length . . . I am become a private citizen on the banks of the Potomac, and under the shadow of my own vine and my own fig-tree, free from the bustle of a camp and the busy scenes of public life, I am solacing myself with those tranquil enjoyments of which the soldier who is ever in pursuit of fame, the statesman whose watchful days and sleepless nights are spent in devising schemes to promote the welfare of his own, perhaps the ruin of other countries, . . . can have very little conception. I am not only retired from all public employments, but I am retiring within myself; and shall be able to view the solitary walk, and tread the paths of private life with heartfelt satisfaction. Envious of none, I am determined to be pleased with all; and this my dear friend, being the order for my march, I will move gently down the stream of life, until I sleep with my fathers."[3]

But the fulfillment of my desire did not come as readily as I had hoped. I was too wound up from war to instantly slip into a quiet domestic life. After I had been home for many months I observed, "I am just beginning to experience that ease and freedom from public cares which, however desirable, takes some time to realize; for strange as it may tell, it is nevertheless true that it was not till lately I could get the better of my usual custom of ruminating, as

1. F 26:463; 1783.
2. F 27:288; 1783.
3. F 27:317; 1783.

soon as I waked in the morning, on the business of the ensuing day; and of my surprise, after having revolved many things in my mind, to find that I was no longer a public man, or had anything to do with public transactions.

"I feel now, however, as I conceive a wearied traveler must do, who, after treading many a painful step with a heavy burden on his shoulders, is eased of the latter, having reached the goal . . . , and from his housetop is looking back and tracing with a grateful eye the meanders by which he escaped the quicksands and mires which lay in his way, and into which none but the All-powerful Guide and Great Disposer of human events could have prevented his falling."[1]

But the peace I had hoped for simply wasn't to be. Four years later I wrote, "I have no wish which aspires beyond the humble and happy lot of living and dying a private citizen on my own farm."[2]

And after I had begun my first term as president I could say with more conviction than ever, "I had rather be at Mount Vernon, with a friend or two about me, than to be attended at the seat of government by the officers of state and the representatives of every power in Europe."[3]

JP: With such strong feelings pulling you back to Mount Vernon, why did you continue to accept appointments elsewhere?

GW: "The consciousness of having discharged that duty which we owe to our country is superior to all other considerations."[4]

JP: Through the lenses of history, you sometimes come across as infallible. Why, then, did you feel unequal to the demands that were placed on you?

---

1. F 27:340; 1784.
2. F 30:42; 1788.
3. F 31:54; 1790.
4. F 29:431; 1788.

GW: When I was appointed commander in chief, I feared that I had "embarked on a tempestuous ocean from whence perhaps no friendly harbor is to be found. . . . It is an honor I by no means aspired to. It is an honor I wished to avoid, as well as from an unwillingness to quit the peaceful enjoyment of my family as from a thorough conviction of my own incapacity and want of experience in the conduct of so momentous a concern; but the partiality of the Congress . . . left me without a choice. May God grant, therefore, that my acceptance of it, may be attended with some good to the common cause. . . . I can answer but for three things: a firm belief of the justice of our cause, close attention in the prosecution of it, and the strictest integrity. If these cannot supply the place of ability and experience, the cause will suffer, and more than probably my character along with it, as reputation derives its principal support from success."[1]

Three years later I noted that "neither interested nor ambitious views led me into the service. I did not solicit the command, but accepted it after much entreaty, with all that diffidence which a conscious want of ability and experience equal to the discharge of so important a trust must naturally create in a mind not quite devoid of thought." But once I began my service, I "pursued the great line of my duty and the object in view (as far as my judgment could direct) as pointedly as the needle to the pole." If however, "the public gets dissatisfied with my services, or a person is found better qualified to answer her expectation, I shall quit the helm with as much satisfaction, and retire to a private station with as much content, as ever the wearied pilgrim felt upon his safe arrival in the Holy Land." If that day were to come, I wished "most devoutly that those who come after may meet with more prosperous gales than I have done, and less difficulty."[2]

---

1. F 3:296–97; 1775.
2. F 10:338; 1778.

JP: Did you have similar hesitations in accepting the presidency of the United States?

GW: Oh, yes! I considered the possibility of being elected president a "dreaded dilemma"—to be called back into public service right when I had expected "to pass an unclouded evening after the stormy day of life, in the bosom of domestic tranquility." I wrote that "I have always felt a kind of gloom upon my mind" whenever I thought I might be so elected and added, "If I should receive the appointment and if I should be prevailed upon to accept it, the acceptance would be attended with more diffidence and reluctance that I ever experienced before in my life."[1]

After I was elected, I admitted candidly that "my movements to the chair of government will be accompanied by feelings not unlike those of a culprit who is going to the place of his execution: so unwilling am I, in the evening of a life nearly consumed in public cares, to quit a peaceful abode for an ocean of difficulties, without that competency of political skill, abilities and inclination which is necessary to manage the helm. . . . Integrity and firmness is all I can promise; these, be the voyage long or short, never shall forsake me although I may be deserted by all men. For of the consolations which are to be derived from these (under any circumstances) the world cannot deprive me."[2]

A few months later, when I was just getting started as president, I confided to Edward Rutledge, who was the youngest signer of the Declaration of Independence and who subsequently fought in the Revolutionary War: "Though I flatter myself the world will do me the justice to believe that, at my time of life and in my circumstances, nothing but a conviction of duty could have induced me to depart from my resolution of remaining in retirement, yet I greatly apprehend that my countrymen will expect too much from me. I fear, if the issue of public measures should not correspond with their sanguine expectations, they

---

1. F 30:111; 1788.
2. F 30:268; 1789.

will turn the extravagant (and I may say undue) praises which they are heaping upon me at this moment, into equally extravagant (though I will fondly hope unmerited) censures. So much is expected, so many untoward circumstances may intervene in such a new and critical situation, that I feel an insuperable diffidence in my own abilities. I feel, in the execution of the duties of my arduous office, how much I shall stand in need of the countenance and aid of every friend to myself, of every friend to the revolution, and of every lover of good government."[1]

JP: Nowadays the President of the United States is a frequent target of a great deal of criticism. Was that your experience? You mention you feared "extravagant . . . censures." Were your countrymen generous when you made mistakes? Or did they heap censures on your head?

GW: Before I began my service I said that it "would be the greatest sacrifice of my personal feelings and wishes that ever I have been called upon to make. It would be to forego repose and domestic enjoyment, for trouble, perhaps for public obloquy: for I should consider myself as entering upon an unexplored field, enveloped on every side with clouds and darkness."[2]

"I anticipated, in a heart filled with distress, the ten thousand embarrassments, perplexities and troubles to which I must again be exposed in the evening of a life, already nearly consumed in public cares."[3]

I'm afraid that trouble and obloquy did follow. Even with the fears I expressed at the beginning of my presidency, "I had no conception that parties would, or even could, go the length I have been witness to; nor did I believe, until lately, that it was within the bonds of probability, hardly within those of possibility, that, while I was using my utmost exertions to establish a [strong] . . .

---

1. F 30:309; 1789.
2. F 30:119; 1788.
3. F 30:238; 1789.

nation . . . , every act of my administration would be tortured, and the grossest, and most insidious misrepresentations of them be made (by giving one side *only* of a subject, and that too in such exaggerated and indecent terms as could scarcely be applied to a Nero; a notorious defaulter; or even to a common pickpocket)."[1]

In my Farewell Address, I observed that I had served "under circumstances in which the passions agitated in every direction were liable to mislead, amidst appearances sometimes dubious, vicissitudes of fortune often discouraging, in situations in which not infrequently want of success has countenanced the spirit of criticism."[2]

In all this I have had one consolation. Even though I have experienced criticisms and misrepresentations from some, others have been most gracious in their support. I feel to acknowledge "that debt of gratitude which I owe to my beloved country for the many honors it has conferred upon me; still more for the steadfast confidence with which it has supported me; and for the opportunities I have thence enjoyed of manifesting my inviolable attachment, by services faithful and persevering, though in usefulness unequal to my zeal. If benefits have resulted to our country from these services, let it always be remembered to your praise, and as an instructive example in our annals, that . . . the constancy of your support was the essential prop of the efforts, and a guarantee of the plans by which they were effected."[3]

"Having performed duties (which I conceive every country has a right to require of its citizens), I claim no merit; but no man can feel more sensibly the reward of approbation for such services, than I do. Next to the consciousness of having acted faithfully in discharging the several trusts to which I have been called, the

---

1. F 35:120; 1796.
2. F 35:217; 1796.
3. F 35:217; 1796.

thanks of one's country, and the esteem of good men, is the highest gratification my mind is susceptible of."[1]

---

1. F 35:493; 1797.

George Washington Before the Battle of Trenton, by John Trumbull, about 1792

2

The Revolutionary War

JP: You seemed to be single-minded in your quest for liberty.

GW: "A people contending for life and liberty are seldom disposed to look with a favorable eye upon either men or measures whose passions, interests or consequences will clash with those inestimable objects."[1]

But even liberty must have boundaries or limits. "Liberty, when it degenerates into licentiousness, begets confusion, and frequently ends in tyranny or some woeful catastrophe."[2]

JP: How do you feel about the efforts of other nations to gain liberty?

GW: "My anxious recollections, my sympathetic feeling, and my best wishes are irresistibly excited whensoever, in any country, I see an oppressed nation unfurl the banners of freedom."[3]

JP: The opposite of liberty is often identified as tyranny. But you sometimes called it something else.

GW: Yes, I called it slavery. "The hour is fast approaching, on which the honor and success of this army, and the safety of our bleeding country depend," I told the troops in 1776. "Remember,

---

1. F 3:361; 1775.
2. F 27:12; 1783.
3. F 34:413; 1796.

officers and soldiers, that you are freemen, fighting for the blessings of liberty—that slavery will be your portion, and that of your
posterity, if you do not acquit yourselves like men."[1]

When I wrote a letter about the battle of Concord, I used the
same thought: "Unhappy it is . . . to reflect that a brother's sword
has been sheathed in a brother's breast, and that the once happy
and peaceful plains of America are either to be drenched with
blood or inhabited by slaves. Sad alternative! But can a virtuous
man hesitate in his choice?"[2]

JP: During the Revolutionary War, you were fighting not just
for change but for independence. Why the more drastic separa-
tion from Great Britain?

GW: I recorded in 1778: "Nothing short of independence, it appears to me, can possibly do. A peace on other terms would, if I
may be allowed the expression, be a peace of war. The injuries we
have received from the British nation were so unprovoked, and
have been so great and so many, that they can never be forgotten.
Besides the feuds, the jealousies, the animosities that would ever
attain a union with them; besides the importance, the advantages,
we should derive from an unrestricted commerce; our fidelity as
a people, our gratitude, our character as men, are opposed to a
coalition with them as subjects, but in case of the last extremity. Were we easily to accede to terms of dependence, no nation,
upon future occasions, let the oppressions of Britain be never
so flagrant and unjust, would interpose for our relief; or, at most,
they would do it with a cautious reluctance, and upon conditions
most probably that would be hard, if not dishonorable to us. . . .
A wise and virtuous perseverance would, and I trust will, free
us entirely."[3]

---

1. F 5:479; 1776.
2. F 3:292; 1775.
3. F 11:289–90; 1778.

JP: I understand you used freedom as a motivation for your men to be bold in battle.

GW: Yes, I did. I encouraged them in 1776: "The time is now near at hand which must probably determine whether Americans are to be freemen or slaves; whether they are to have any property they can call their own; whether their houses and farms are to be pillaged and destroyed, and they consigned to a state of wretchedness from which no human efforts will deliver them. The fate of unborn millions will now depend, under God, on the courage and conduct of this army. Our cruel and unrelenting enemy leaves us no choice but a brave resistance, or the most abject submission. . . . We have, therefore, to resolve to conquer or die."[1]

In 1777 I added: "Let it never be said that, in a day of action, you turned your backs on the foe; let the enemy no longer triumph. They brand you with ignominious epithets. Will you patiently endure that reproach? Will you suffer the wounds given to your country to go unrevenged? Will you resign your parents, wives, children and friends to be the wretched vassals of a proud, insulting foe? And your own necks to the halter? . . . Nothing then remains, but nobly to contend for all that is dear to us. Every motive that can touch the human breast calls us to the most vigorous exertions. Our dearest rights, our dearest friends, and our own lives, honor, glory and even shame, urge us to the fight. And my fellow soldiers! when an opportunity presents, be firm, be brave; show yourselves men, and victory is yours."[2]

JP: How did you justify lifting up arms to defend your liberty?

GW: "At a time when our lordly masters in Great Britain will be satisfied with nothing less than the deprivation of American freedom, it seems highly necessary that something should be done to avert the stroke and maintain the liberty which we

---

1. F 5:211; 1776.
2. F 9:306; 1777.

have derived from our ancestors. But the manner of doing it, to answer the purpose effectually, is the point in question. That no man should scruple, or hesitate a moment, to use arms in defense of so valuable a blessing, on which all the good and evil of life depends, is clearly my opinion. Yet arms, I would beg leave to add, should be the last resource, the *dernier resort*. Addresses to the throne, and remonstrances to parliament, we have already . . . proved the inefficacy of."[1]

JP: How did you express your motives in going to war?

GW: "The Honor and safety of our bleeding country, and every other motive that can influence the brave and heroic patriot, call loudly upon us, to acquit ourselves with spirit. In short, we must now determine to be enslaved or free. If we make freedom our choice, we must obtain it, by the blessing of Heaven on our united and vigorous efforts."[2]

A year earlier I put it a different way, looking toward our posterity—and the blessings we had received from those who came before: "Under [God's] Providence, those who influence the councils of America, and all the other inhabitants of the united colonies at the hazard of their lives are determined to hand down to posterity those just and invaluable privileges, which they received from their ancestors."[3]

And in a circular to the states sent at the end of the war, I observed, "It is yet to be decided whether the revolution must ultimately be considered as a blessing or a curse: a blessing or a curse, not to the present age alone, for with our fate will the destiny of unborn millions be involved."[4]

---

1. F 2:501; 1769.
2. F 5:398; 1776.
3. F 3:431; 1775.
4. F 26:486; 1783.

JP: What was the secret to your success in the war—which you won against all odds?

GW: "If we had a secret resource of a nature unknown to our enemy, it was in the unconquerable resolution of our citizens, the conscious rectitude of our cause, and a confident trust that we should not be forsaken by Heaven."[1]

JP: As the war progressed, discouragement must surely have set in.

GW: I noted that "friends and foes seem now to combine to pull down the goodly fabric we have hitherto been raising at the expense of so much time, blood, and treasure; and unless the bodies politick will exert themselves to bring things back to first principles, correct abuses, and punish our internal foes, inevitable ruin must follow. Indeed we seem to be verging so fast to destruction that I am filled with sensations to which I have been a stranger till within these three months. Our enemy behold with exultation and joy how effectually we labor for their benefit; and from being in a state of absolute despair, and on the point of evacuating America, are now on tiptoe; nothing therefore in my judgment can save us but a total reformation in our own conduct, or some decisive turn to affairs in Europe. The former alas! to our shame be it spoken! is less likely to happen than the latter, as it is now consistent with the views of the speculators, various tribes of money makers, and stock jobbers of all denominations to continue the war for their own private emolument, without considering that their avarice, and thirst for gain must plunge everything (including themselves) in one common ruin."[2]

JP: I understand that the sufferings of the troops during the Revolutionary War were almost indescribable.

---

1. F 30:297; 1789.
2. F 14:300; 1779.

GW: Their conditions were so abhorrent that I addressed it often in my correspondence.

In 1776: "I believe I may with great truth affirm that no man perhaps since the first institution of armies ever commanded one under more difficult circumstances than I have done. To enumerate the particulars would fill a volume. Many of the difficulties and distresses were of so peculiar a cast that, in order to conceal them from the enemy, I was obliged to conceal them from my friends, and indeed from my own army, thereby subjecting my conduct to interpretations unfavorable to my character, especially by those at a distance who could not in the smallest degree be acquainted with the springs that governed it."[1]

In 1777: "Unless some great and capital change suddenly takes place . . . , this army must inevitably be reduced to one or other of these three things. Starve, dissolve, or disperse, in order to obtain subsistence in the best manner they can. . . . Three or four days bad weather would prove our destruction. What then is to become of the army this winter? and if we are as often without provisions now, as with [them], what is to become of us in the spring, when our force will be collected, with the aid perhaps of militia, to take advantage of an early campaign before the enemy can be reinforced? . . .

"Few men [have] more than one shirt, many only the [half] of one, and some none at all. . . . Besides a number of men confined to hospitals . . . , we have . . . no less than 2898 men now in camp unfit for duty because they are bare foot and otherwise naked. . . . Notwithstanding which, . . . we find gentlemen . . . reprobating the measure [of putting the army into winter quarters] as much as if they thought men [the soldiery] were made of stocks or stones and equally insensible of frost and snow and moreover, as if they conceived it [easily] practicable for an inferior army under the disadvantages I have described . . . to confine a

---

1. F 4:450; 1776.

superior one (in all respects well appointed, and provided for a winters campaign) within the city of Philadelphia, and [to] cover from depredation and waste the states of Pennsylvania., Jersey, etc., but what makes this matter still more extraordinary in my eye is that these very gentlemen. who were well apprised of the nakedness of the troops, . . . should think a winter's campaign and the covering these states from the invasion of an enemy so easy [and practicable] a business. I can assure those gentlemen that it is a much easier and less distressing thing to draw remonstrances in a comfortable room by a good fire side than to occupy a cold bleak hill and sleep under frost and snow without clothes or blankets; however, although they seem to have little feeling for the naked, and distressed soldier[s], I feel superabundantly for them, and from my soul pity those miseries, which it is neither in my power to relieve or prevent.

"It is for these reasons therefore I have dwelt upon the subject, and it adds not a little to my other difficulties, and distress, to find that much more is expected of me than is possible to be performed, and that upon the ground of safety and policy, I am obliged to conceal the true state of the army from public view and thereby expose myself to detraction and calumny."[1]

Later that same year: "Soap is another article in great demand—the Continental allowance is too small, and dear, as every necessary of life is now got, a soldier's pay will not enable him to purchase, by which means his consequent dirtiness adds not a little to the disease of the Army."[2]

And again: "Our sick naked, our well naked, our unfortunate men in captivity naked!"[3]

In 1778: "The soldiers . . . have been (two or three times), days together, without provisions; and once six days without any of the meat kind; could the poor horses tell their tale, it would be

---

1. F 10:192; 1777.
2. F 8:441; 1777.
3. F 10:233; 1777.

in a strain still more lamentable, as numbers have actually died from pure want."[1]

And later that same year: "Without arrogance or the smallest deviation from truth it may be said that no history now extant can furnish an instance of an army's suffering such uncommon hardships as ours has done, and bearing them with the same patience and fortitude. To see men, without clothes to cover their nakedness, without blankets to lie on, without shoes, by which their marches might be traced by blood from their feet, and almost as often without provisions as with them, marching through the frost and snow, and at Christmas taking up their winter-quarters within a day's march of the enemy, without a house or hut to cover them, till they could be built, and submitting to it without a murmur, is a proof of patience and obedience, which in my opinion can scarce be paralleled."[2]

In 1783: "If historiographers should be hardy enough to fill the page of history with the advantages that have been gained with unequal numbers, on the part of America, in the course of this contest, and attempt to relate the distressing circumstances under which they have been obtained it is more than probable that posterity will bestow on their labors the epithet and marks of fiction; for it will not be believed that such a force as Great Britain has employed for eight years in this country could be baffled in their plan of subjugating it by numbers infinitely less, composed of men oftentimes half starved; always in rags, without pay, and experiencing, at times, every species of distress which human nature is capable of undergoing."[3]

I wish I hadn't been required to focus so much on such difficult things. But "painful as the task is to describe the dark side

1. F 11:117; 1778.
2. F 11:291–92; 1778.
3. F 26:104; 1783.

of our affairs, it sometimes becomes a matter of indispensable necessity."[1]

Unfortunately, "military arrangements, and movements in consequence, like the mechanism of a clock, will be imperfect and disordered by the want of a part."[2]

JP: How did you treat prisoners of war?

GW: When I transported prisoners during the French and Indian War, "I . . . showed all the respect I could to them . . . , and [gave] some necessary clothing, by which I have disfurnished myself."[3]

JP: What instructions did you give about the treatment of prisoners of war during the Revolutionary War?

GW: I told my men, "Any other prisoners who may fall into your hands, you will treat with as much humanity and kindness, as may be consistent with your own safety and the public Interest."[4]

Later, I added, "It is not my wish that severity should be exercised towards any, whom the fortune of war has thrown, or, shall throw into our hands. On the contrary, It is my desire that the utmost humanity should be shown them. I am convinced the latter has been the prevailing line of conduct to prisoners."[5]

JP: You mention your concern about speculators, those who sought to get rich from the war. Did you condemn them?

GW: "I [could] not, with any degree of patience, behold the infamous practices of speculators, monopolizers, and all that class of gentry which [were] preying upon our very vitals, and, for the

---

1. F 25:226; 1782.
2. F 10:197; 1777.
3. F 1:67; 1754.
4. F 3:494; 1771.
5. F 6:620; 1776.

sake of a little dirty pelf, [were] putting the rights and liberties of the country into the most imminent danger."[1]

JP: You have been clear that you felt that God assisted in America's victory in the war.

GW: It was indeed clear to me. "The disadvantageous circumstances on our part, under which the war was undertaken, can never be forgotten. The singular interpositions of Providence in our feeble condition were such, as could scarcely escape the attention of the most unobserving; while the unparalleled perseverance of the armies of the United States, through almost every possible suffering and discouragement for the space of eight long years, was little short of a standing miracle."[2]

During the 1776 siege of Boston I observed: "If I shall be able to rise superior to these [present challenges], and many other difficulties which might be enumerated, I shall most religiously believe that the finger of Providence is in it."[3]

JP: How did you thank and encourage your troops at the end of the war?

GW: "While the general recollects the almost infinite variety of scenes through which we have passed, with a mixture of pleasure, astonishment, and gratitude; while he contemplates the prospects before us with rapture; he cannot help wishing that all the brave men . . . who have shared in the toils and dangers of effecting this glorious revolution, of rescuing millions from the hand of oppression, and of laying the foundation of a great empire, might be impressed with a proper idea of the dignified part they have been called to act (under the smiles of providence) on the stage of human affairs: for, happy, thrice happy shall they be pronounced hereafter, who have contributed anything, who have performed

---

1. F 15:180; 1779.
2. F 27:223; 1783.
3. F 4:243; 1776.

the meanest office in erecting this stupendous *fabric* of *freedom* and *empire* on the broad basis of independency; who have assisted in protecting the rights of human nature and establishing an asylum for the poor and oppressed of all nations and religions.

"The glorious task for which we first flew to arms being thus accomplished, the liberties of our country being fully acknowledged, and firmly secured by the smiles of heaven, on the purity of our cause, and the honest exertions of a feeble people (determined to be free) against a powerful nation (disposed to oppress them) and the character of those who have persevered, through every extremity of hardship; suffering and danger being immortalized by the illustrious appellation of the *patriot army:* Nothing now remains but for the actors of this mighty scene to preserve a perfect, unvarying, consistency of character through the very last act; to close the drama with applause; and to retire from the military theatre with the same approbation of angels and men which have crowned all their former virtuous actions."[1]

I added in another setting, "Nor would I rob the fairer sex of their share in the glory of a revolution so honorable to human nature, for, indeed, I think . . . ladies are in the number of the best patriots America can boast."[2]

JP: What were your feelings at the end of the war?

GW: I expressed those feelings plainly: "I pant for retirement. . . . I can truly say that the first wish of my soul is to return speedily into the bosom of that country which gave me birth and in the sweet enjoyment of domestic pleasures and the company of a few friends to end my days in quiet when I shall be called from this stage."[3]

"I only wait (and with anxious impatience) the arrival of the definitive treaty, that I may take leave of my military employments

---

1. F 26:335; 1783.
2. F 30:76; 1788.
3. F 24:347; 1782.

and by bidding adieu to public life, forever, enjoy the shades of retirement that ease and tranquility to which, for more than eight years, I have been an entire stranger and for which a mind which has been constantly on the stretch during that period and perplexed with a thousand embarrassing circumstances, oftentimes without ray of light to guide it; stands much in need."[1]

JP: Let's talk about armies in general. How important is the character of soldiers?

GW: Very. For example, in orders to the army, I once said: "The blessing and protection of Heaven are at all times necessary but especially so in times of public distress and danger—The general hopes and trusts that every officer and man, will endeavor so to live, and act, as becomes a Christian soldier defending the dearest rights and liberties of his country."[2]

JP: What is required for an army to be successful?

GW: "Discipline is the soul of an army. It makes small numbers formidable; procures success to the weak, and esteem to all."[3]

And: "Nothing can be more hurtful to the service, than the neglect of discipline; for that discipline, more than numbers, gives one army the superiority over another."[4]

Further: "An army formed of good officers moves like clockwork; but there is no situation upon earth less enviable, nor more distressing, than that person's who is at the head of troops which are regardless of order and discipline."[5]

Finally: "It is infinitely better to have a *few* good men than *many* indifferent ones."[6]

---

1. F 27:89; 1783.
2. F 5:244–45; 1776.
3. F 2:114; 1757.
4. F 8:359; 1777.
5. F 6:115; 1776.
6. F 36:403; 1798.

JP: Should members of the military view themselves as being of a different class from the rest of the citizenry?

GW: "When we assumed the soldier, we did not lay aside the citizen; and we shall most sincerely rejoice with you in the happy hour when the establishment of American liberty, upon the most firm and solid foundations shall enable us to return to our private stations in the bosom of a free, peacefully and happy country."[1]

During the Revolutionary War, I wrote further on this by saying, "Let us therefore animate and encourage each other, and show the whole world that a freeman, contending for liberty on his own ground, is superior to any slavish mercenary on earth."[2]

JP: Some by their actions seem to suggest that the military should serve from patriotic duty and that the troops shouldn't worry much about pay.

GW: We dealt with this very issue, repeatedly, during our great war. Regardless of patriotic interests, "something is due to the man who puts his life in his hands, hazards his health, and forsakes the sweets of domestic enjoyments."[3]

JP: Do you feel it very important for citizens to serve their country in some way?

GW: "It is a maxim with me that in times of imminent danger to a country, every true patriot should occupy the post in which he can render his services to his country the most effectually."[4]

JP: Standing armies can be dangerous to a country's freedom. Are they worth the risk?

GW: "Had we formed a permanent army in the beginning, which, by the continuance of the same men in service, had been

---

1. F 3:305; 1775.
2. F 5:211; 1776.
3. F 6:107–8; 1776.
4. F 37:136; 1799.

capable of discipline, we never should have had to retreat with
a handful of men across the Delaware in '76, trembling for the
fate of America, which nothing but the infatuation of the enemy
could have saved; we should not have remained all the succeed-
ing winter at their mercy, with sometimes scarcely a sufficient
body of men to mount the ordinary guards, liable at every moment to be dissipated, if they had only thought proper to march
against us; we should not have been under the necessity of fighting at Brandywine, with an unequal number of raw troops, and
afterwards of seeing Philadelphia fall a prey to a victorious army;
we should not have been at Valley Forge with less than half the
force of the enemy, destitute of everything, in a situation neither
to resist nor to retire; we should not have seen New York left
with a handful of men, yet an overmatch for the main army of
these states, while the principal part of their force was detached
for the reduction of two of them; we should not have found ourselves this spring so weak, as to be insulted by five thousand
men, unable to protect our baggage and magazines, their security depending on a good countenance, and a want of enterprise
in the enemy; we should not have been the greatest part of the
war inferior to the enemy, indebted for our safety to their in-
activity, enduring frequently the mortification of seeing inviting
opportunities to ruin them pass unimproved for want of a force,
which the country was completely able to afford; to see the country ravaged, our towns burnt, the inhabitants plundered, abused,
murdered with impunity from the same cause.

"There is every reason to believe, the war has been protracted
on this account. Our opposition being less, made the successes
of the enemy greater. The fluctuation of the army kept alive their
hopes, and at every period of the dissolution of a considerable
part of it, they have flattered themselves with some decisive advantages. Had we kept a permanent army on foot, the enemy

could have had nothing to hope for, and would in all probability have listened to terms long since."[1]

If we don't have a standing army, then we're reduced to relying wholly on the militia. "To place any dependence upon militia, is, assuredly, resting upon a broken staff. Men just dragged from the tender scenes of domestic life—unaccustomed to the din of arms—totally unacquainted with every kind of military skill, which being followed by a want of confidence in themselves when opposed to troops regularly trained, disciplined, and appointed, superior in knowledge, and superior in arms, makes them timid and ready to fly from their own shadows."[2]

I warned the president of Congress in 1776: "I am persuaded, and as fully convinced as I am of any one fact that has happened, that our liberties must of necessity be greatly hazarded, if not entirely lost, if their defense is left to any but a permanent standing army; I mean, one to exist during the war. Nor would the expense, incident to the support of such a body of troops, as would be competent to almost every exigency, far exceed that, which is daily incurred by calling in succor, and new enlistments, which, when effected, are not attended with any good consequences. Men, who have been free and subject to no control, cannot be reduced to order in an instant; and the privileges and exemptions they claim and will have influence the conduct of others; and the aid derived from them is nearly counterbalanced by the disorder, irregularity, and confusion they occasion."[3]

JP: With all the experience you had with leading an army, do you have any other counsel for us?

GW: The most important thing I would say is to be united. I emphasized this to Major General Philip Schuyler during the Revolutionary War, "Enjoin this upon the officers, and let them

1. F 19:408–10; 1780.
2. F 6:110; 1776.
3. F 6:5–6; 1776.

inculcate, and press home to the soldiery, the necessity of order and harmony among them, who are embarked in one common cause, and mutually contending for all that freemen hold dear. I am persuaded, if the officers will but exert themselves, these animosities, this disorder, will in a great measure subside, and nothing being more essential to the service than that it should, I am hopeful nothing on their parts will be wanting to effect it."[1]

Twenty years later, as commander in chief, I repeated this observation to General Henry Knox, "My first wish would be that my military family and the whole army should consider themselves as a band of brothers, willing and ready to die for each other."[2]

---

1. F 5:290–91; 1776.
2. F 36:508; 1798.

Washington at the Constitutional Convention of 1787,
by Junius Brutus Stearns, 1856

3

The Constitution

JP: Tell us about your regard for the Constitution.

GW: I called it "the best fabric of human government and happiness that has ever seen presented for the acceptance of mankind."[1]

And it was ever my prayer "that your union and brotherly affection may be perpetual; that the free constitution, which is the work of your hands, may be sacredly maintained; that its administration in every department may be stamped with wisdom and virtue; that, in fine, the happiness of the people of these states, under the auspices of liberty, may be made complete, by so careful a preservation and so prudent a use of this blessing as will acquire to them the glory of recommending it to the applause, the affection, and adoption of every nation which is yet a stranger to it."[2]

JP: Did you feel that God's hand was evident in the establishment of the Constitution?

GW: "It appear[ed] to me . . . little short of a miracle that the delegates from so many different states . . . should unite in forming a system of national government."[3]

---

1. F 33:475; 1794.
2. F 35:217; 1796.
3. F 29:409–10; 1788.

I saw God's hand in both the creation and the ratification of the Constitution:

"We may, with a kind of grateful and pious exultation," I wrote, "trace the finger of Providence through those dark and mysterious events, which first induced the states to appoint a general convention and then led them one after another . . . into an adoption of the system recommended by that general convention; thereby, in all human probability, laying a lasting foundation for tranquility and happiness; when we had but too much reason to fear that confusion and misery were coming rapidly upon us. That the same good Providence may still continue to protect us and prevent us from dashing the cup of national felicity just as it has been lifted to our lips, is [my] earnest prayer."[1]

Near the beginning of the Constitutional Convention, I said, "If to please the people, we offer what we ourselves disapprove, how can we afterwards defend our work? Let us raise a standard to which the wise and the honest can repair. The event is in the hand of God."[2]

While the Constitution was being ratified, I foresaw that "should everything proceed with harmony and consent according to our actual wishes and expectations, . . . it will be so much beyond anything we had a right to imagine or expect eighteen months ago, that it will demonstrate as visibly the finger of Providence, as any possible event in the course of human affairs can ever designate it. It is impracticable for you or anyone who has not been on the spot, to realize the change in men's minds and the progress towards rectitude in thinking and acting which will then have been made."[3]

And, "No one *can* rejoice more than I do at every step the people of this great country take to preserve the union, establish good order and government, and to render the nation happy at

---

1. F 30:22; 1788.
2. Farrand, 3:382; 1787.
3. F 29:507–8; 1788.

home and respectable abroad. No country upon earth ever had it more in its power to attain these blessings than united America. Wondrously strange then, and much to be regretted indeed would it be, were we to neglect the means, and to depart from the road which Providence has pointed us to, so plainly; I cannot believe it will ever come to pass. The great Governor of the Universe has led us too long and too far on the road to happiness and glory, to forsake us in the midst of it."[1]

Later I added, writing to another correspondent, "That invisible hand which has so often interposed to save our country from impending destruction, seems in no instance to have been more remarkably excited than in that of disposing the people of this extensive continent to adopt, in a peaceable manner, a Constitution, which if well administered, bids fair to make America a happy nation."[2]

JP: Did you consider the Constitution to be perfectly formed then?

GW: Others have asked the same question. I wrote to Patrick Henry, "I wish the constitution, which is offered, had been made more perfect; but I sincerely believe it is the best that could be obtained at this time. And, as a constitutional door is opened for amendment hereafter, the adoption of it, under the present circumstances of the union, is in my opinion desirable."[3]

Six weeks later I told my nephew Bushrod Washington that "the warmest friends and the best supports the constitution has, do not contend that it is free from imperfections; but they found them unavoidable, and are sensible, if evil is likely to arise therefrom, the remedy must come hereafter; for in the present moment it is not to be obtained; and, as there is a constitutional door open for it, I think the people (for it is with them to judge), can, as they

---

1. F 30:11; 1788.
2. F 30:317; 1789.
3. F 29:278; 1787.

will have the advantage of experience on their side, decide with as much propriety on the alterations and amendments which are necessary, as ourselves. I do not think we are more inspired, have more wisdom, or possess more virtue, than those who will come after us."[1]

JP: But again and again the Constitution has been changed without the citizens of the nation going through the formal amendment process.

GW: In my farewell address, I cautioned, "Towards the preservation of your government and the permanency of your present happy state, it is requisite, not only that you steadily discountenance irregular oppositions to its acknowledged authority, but also that you resist with care the spirit of innovation upon its principles however specious the pretexts. One method of assault may be to effect, in the forms of the Constitution, alterations which will impair the energy of the system, and thus to undermine what cannot be directly overthrown."[2]

In that same speech I said, "The basis of our political systems is the right of the people to make and to alter their constitutions of government. But the constitution which at any time exists, till changed by an explicit and authentic act of the whole people, is sacredly obligatory upon all. The very idea of the power and the right of the people to establish government presupposes the duty of every individual to obey the established government."[3]

"If in the opinion of the people, the distribution or modification of the constitutional powers be in any particular wrong, let it be corrected by an amendment in the way which the Constitution designates. But let there be no change by usurpation; for though

1. F 29:311; 1787.
2. F 35:225; 1796.
3. F 35:224; 1796.

this, in one instance, may be the instrument of good, it is the customary weapon by which free governments are destroyed."[1]

I also cautioned that we should be careful in making changes: "In all the changes to which you may be invited, remember that time and habit are at least as necessary to fix the true character of governments, as of other human institutions; that experience is the surest standard, by which to test the real tendency of the existing Constitution of a country; that facility in changes upon the credit of mere hypotheses and opinion exposes to perpetual change, from the endless variety of hypotheses and opinion: and remember, especially, that for the efficient management of your common interests, in a country so extensive as ours, a government of as much vigor as is consistent with the perfect security of liberty is indispensable. Liberty itself will find in such a government, with powers properly distributed and adjusted, its surest guardian."[2]

JP: Did you seek to strictly adhere to the requirements and restrictions of the Constitution as president?

GW: I emphasized in 1790, near the beginning of my first term, "The Constitution of the United States, and the laws made under it, must mark the line of my official conduct."[3]

And I repeated the same idea five years later: "The Constitution is the guide which I never will abandon."[4]

I held to these principles even under the Articles of Confederation. I said, "Precedents are dangerous things; let the reins of government then be braced and held with a steady hand, and every violation of the Constitution be reprehended: if defective,

---

1. F 35:229; 1796.
2. F 35:225–26; 1796.
3. F 31:9; 1790.
4. F 34:253; 1795.

let it be amended, but not suffered to be trampled upon whilst it has an existence."[1]

JP: Were you worried that successive generations might not sufficiently value the Constitution?

GW: I had already seen a terrible precedent in the way Christianity was treated. I noted with concern that "the blessed religion revealed in the word of God will remain an eternal and awful monument to prove that the best institution may be abused by human depravity; and that they may even, in some instances be made subservient to the vilest purposes." I then directly applied the concern to the U.S. Constitution: "Should, hereafter, those incited by the lust of power and prompted by the supineness or venality of their constituents, overleap the known barriers of this Constitution and violate the unalienable rights of humanity: it will only serve to show that no compact among men (however provident in its construction and sacred in its ratification) can be pronounced everlasting and inviolable, and if I may so express myself, that no wall of words, that no mound of parchment can be so formed as to stand against the sweeping torrent of boundless ambition on the side, aided by the sapping current of corrupted morals on the other."[2]

JP: Those are impressive and sobering words. The specific threats you outline have proven out: "lust for power" and "boundless ambition" on the part of politicians and, on the part of the citizenry, "supineness," "venality," and "corrupted morals." And I see, again, that you viewed the creation of the Constitution as "provident" and "sacred," thus seeing God's hand in the writing and ratification. Since you considered the Constitution to be an inspired document, did you believe it might have influence on generations to come?

---

1. F 29:34–35; 1786.
2. F 30:301–2; 1789.

GW: Absolutely. During the months of ratification, I predicted, "The plot thickens fast. A few short weeks will determine the political fate of America for the present generation, and probably produce no small influence on the happiness of society through a long succession of ages to come."[1]

JP: Suppose the states had chosen not to ratify the constitution you and your colleagues created in 1787—do you suppose you could simply have gone back to the drawing board?

GW: No. I gave it as my opinion in November 1787 that "should the states reject this excellent Constitution, the probability is, an opportunity will never again offer to cancel another in peace—the next will be drawn in blood."[2]

JP: Did you ever fear that we might lose our new-found freedoms?

GW: As the Constitution was being ratified I said, "By folly and improper conduct, proceeding from a variety of causes, we may now and then get bewildered; but I hope and trust that there is good sense and virtue enough left to recover the right path before we shall be entirely lost."[3]

---

1. F 29:507–8; 1788.
2. *Pennsylvania Journal*, Nov. 14, 1787, p. 3.
3. F 30:11; 1788.

George Washington, by Adolf Wertmuller, 1795

4

The United States and Its Government

JP: How clearly did you see that America was blessed or favored by God?

GW: A draft of my farewell address included a sentence that I felt strongly about: "As the all-wise dispenser of human blessings has favored no nation of the earth with more abundant, and substantial means of happiness than united America, that we may not be so ungrateful to our Creator, so wanting to ourselves; and so regardless of posterity, as to dash the cup of beneficence which is thus bountifully offered to our acceptance."[1]

Years earlier, I shared my belief that God would preserve our new and very vulnerable nation—something he did indeed do. I reflected, "It is indeed a pleasure, from the walks of private life to view in retrospect, all the meanderings of our past labors, the difficulties through which we have waded, and the fortunate haven to which the ship has been brought! Is it possible after this that it should founder? Will not the all wise, and all powerful Director of human events, preserve it? I think he will, he may however (for wise purposes not discoverable by finite minds) suffer our indiscretions and folly to place our national character low in the political scale; and this, unless more wisdom and less prej-

---

1. F 35:56; 1796.

udice take the lead in our governments, will most assuredly be the case."[1]

JP: Why would God take an interest in our small nation?

GW: Because what I expressed during the Revolutionary War was true: "Our cause is noble; it is the cause of mankind!"[2]

JP: So America was established not only for America?

GW: I wrote something in 1788 that I stand by today: "The prospect, that a good general government will in all human probability be soon established in America, affords me more substantial satisfaction than I have ever before derived from any political event. Because there is a rational ground for believing that not only the happiness of my own countrymen, but that of mankind in general, will be promoted by it."[3]

JP: It's clear that you think liberty in America had an effect on the rest of the world.

GW: I said in my first inaugural address, "The preservation of the sacred fire of liberty, and the destiny of the republican model of government, are justly considered as deeply, perhaps as finally staked, on the experiment entrusted to the hands of the American people."[4]

JP: In our time some Americans seem to be selfishly focused only on themselves and their immediate needs. They seem to think there is no problem with that. What would you say to them?

GW: "It should be the highest ambition of every American to extend his views beyond himself, and to bear in mind that his conduct will not only affect himself, his country, and his imme-

---

1. F 27:399; 1784.
2. F 14:313; 1779.
3. F 30:169; 1788.
4. F 30:294–95; 1789.

diate posterity; but that its influence may be co-extensive with the world, and stamp political happiness or misery on ages yet unborn."[1]

JP: Some have said that in our "modern" day we understand things much better than thinkers in your day, that we are much more advanced. Because of that, they suggest we should be willing to change our form of government. How would you respond to that argument?

GW: "The foundation of our empire was not laid in the gloomy age of ignorance and superstition, but at an epoch when the rights of mankind were better understood and more clearly defined, than at any former period, the researches of the human mind, after social happiness, have been carried to a great extent, the treasures of knowledge, acquired by the labors of philosophers, sages and legislatures, through a long succession of years, are laid open for our use, and their collected wisdom may be happily applied in the establishment of our forms of government; the free cultivation of letters, the unbounded extension of commerce, the progressive refinement of manners, the growing liberality of sentiment, and above all, the pure and benign light of revelation, have had ameliorating influence on mankind and increased the blessings of society. At this auspicious period, the United States came into existence as a nation, and if their citizens should not be completely free and happy, the fault will be entirely their own."[2]

JP: How did you describe the freedoms America enjoyed under their new constitution?

GW: "The citizens of the United States of America have the right to applaud themselves for having given to mankind examples of an enlarged and liberal policy worthy of imitation. All possess alike liberty of conscience and immunities of citizen-

1. F 30:385; 1789.
2. F 26:485; 1783.

ship. It is now no more that toleration is spoken of as if it were by the indulgence of one class of citizens that another enjoyed the exercise of their inherent natural rights, for happily the government of the United States, which gives to bigotry no sanction, to persecution no assistance, requires only that they who live under its protection should demean themselves as good citizens in giving it on all occasions their effectual support."[1]

JP: What would you say is the foundation of our freedom?

GW: "I always believed that an unequivocally free and equal representation of the people in the legislature, together with an efficient and responsible executive, were the great pillars on which the preservation of American freedom must depend."[2]

JP: How is our government designed to protect our freedom?

GW: "With regard to the two great points [of good government] (the pivots upon which the whole machine must move,) my creed is simply,

"1st. That the general government is not invested with more powers than are indispensably necessary to perform the functions of a good government; and, consequently, that no objection ought to be made against the quantity of power delegated to it.

"21y. That these powers (as the appointment of all rulers will forever arise from, and, at short stated intervals, recur to the free suffrage of the people) are so distributed among the legislative, executive, and judicial branches, into which the general government is arranged, that it can never be in danger of degenerating into a monarchy, an oligarchy, an aristocracy, or any other despotic or oppressive form, so long as there shall remain any virtue in the body of the people.

" . . . It will at least be a recommendation to the proposed Constitution that it is provided with more checks and barriers

---

1. Abbot, 6:284–86; 1790.
2. F 30:496; 1790.

against the introduction of tyranny, and those of a nature less liable to be surmounted, than any government hitherto instituted among mortals, hath possessed."[1]

JP: How did you view the prospects of the new nation of America?

GW: In 1795, I shared my vision of that very issue. I said, "Every part of the union displays indications of rapid and various improvement, and with burdens so light as scarcely to be perceived; with resources fully adequate to our present exigencies; with governments founded on genuine principles of rational liberty, and with mild and wholesome laws; is it too much to say, that our country exhibits a spectacle of national happiness never surpassed if ever before equaled?

"Placed in a situation every way so auspicious, motives of commanding force impel us, with sincere acknowledgment to heaven, and pure love to our country, to unite our efforts to preserve, prolong, and improve, our immense advantages."[2]

Then in 1798, only a little more than a year before I died, I added: "The citizens of America, placed in the most enviable condition, as the sole lords and proprietors of a vast tract of continent, comprehending all the various soils and climates of the world, and abounding with all the necessaries and conveniences of life, are . . . acknowledged to be possessed of absolute freedom and independency; they are, from this period, to be considered as the actors on a most conspicuous theatre, which seems to be peculiarly designated by Providence for the display of human greatness and felicity; here, they are not only surrounded with everything which can contribute to the completion of private and domestic enjoyment, but Heaven has crowned all its other bless-

---

1. F 29:410–11; 1788.
2. F 34:389; 1795.

ings, by giving a fairer opportunity for political happiness, than any other nation has ever been favored with."[1]

JP: How important do you feel it is that the federal government be successful?

GW: "I consider the successful administration of the general government as an object of almost infinite consequence to the present and future happiness of the citizens of the United States."[2]

JP: Which do you feel should be dominant—the federal government or the states?

GW: "We are known by no other character among nations than as the United States; Massachusetts or Virginia is no better defined, nor any more thought of by foreign powers than the county of Worcester in Massachusetts is by Virginia, or Glouster County in Virginia is by Massachusetts (respectable as they are); and yet these counties, with as much propriety might oppose themselves to the laws of the state in which they are, as an individual state can oppose itself to the federal government, by which it is, or ought to be bound. Each of these counties has, no doubt, its local polity and interests. These should be attended to, and brought before their respective legislatures with all the force their importance merits; but when they come in contact with the general interest of the state; when superior considerations preponderate in favor of the whole, their voices should be heard no more; so should it be with individual states when compared to the union. Otherwise I think it may properly be asked for what purpose do we farcically pretend to be united?

"Why do Congress spend months together in deliberating upon, debating, and digesting plans, which are made as palatable, and as wholesome to the Constitution of this country as

1. F 26:484–85; 1798.
2. F 30:510; 1789.

the nature of things will admit of, when some states will pay no attention to them, and others regard them but partially; by which means all those evils which proceed from delay, are felt by the whole; while the compliant states are not only suffering by these neglects, but in many instances are injured most capitally by their own exertions; which are wasted for want of the united effort. . . . In a word, I think the blood and treasure which has been spent in it has been lavished to little purpose, unless we can be better cemented."[1]

JP: How would you describe the relationship of the states to the greater union?

GW: "To me, it appears no unjust simile to compare the affairs of this great Continent to the mechanism of a clock, each state representing some one or other of the smaller parts of it which they are endeavoring to put in fine order without considering how useless and unavailing their labor is unless the great wheel or spring which is to set the whole in motion is also well attended to and kept in good order."[2]

JP: Under the Articles of Confederation, the states seemed to have little unity and the central government had little strength. What could be done to ensure the freedom and happiness of Americans?

GW: I talked about this problem while we were indeed still under the Articles of Confederation: "Unless the states will suffer Congress to exercise those prerogatives, they are undoubtedly invested with by the Constitution, everything must very rapidly tend to anarchy and confusion. . . . It is indispensable to the happiness of the individual states that there should be lodged, somewhere, a supreme power to regulate and govern the general concerns of the confederated republic, without which the union

---

1. F 27:50–51; 1783.
2. F 14:301; 1779.

cannot be of long duration. . . . There must be a faithful and pointed compliance on the part of every state, with the late proposals and demands of Congress, or the most fatal consequences will ensue. Unless we can be enabled by the concurrence of the states, to participate of the fruits of the revolution, and enjoy the essential benefits of civil society, under a form of government so free and uncorrupted, so happily guarded against the danger of oppression, as has been devised and adopted by the Articles of Confederation, it will be a subject of regret that so much blood and treasure have been lavished for no purpose, that so many sufferings have been encountered without a compensation, and that so many sacrifices have been made in vain."[1]

JP: Also, the Articles of Confederation gave us a very weak federal government. How dangerous was our situation without more authority on the national level?

GW: I observed then: "We are certainly in a delicate situation, but my fear is that the people are not yet sufficiently *misled* to retract from error. To be plainer, I think there is more wickedness than ignorance mixed in our councils. Under this impression, I scarcely know what opinion to entertain of a general convention. That it is necessary to revise and amend the articles of confederation, I entertain *no* doubt; but what may be the consequences of such an attempt is doubtful. Yet something must be done, or the fabric must fall, for it certainly is tottering.

"Ignorance and design are difficult to combat. Out of these proceed illiberal sentiments, *improper* jealousies, and a train of evils which oftentimes, in republican governments, must be sorely felt before they can be removed. The former, that is ignorance, being a fit soil for the latter to work in, tools are employed by them which a generous mind would disdain to use; and which nothing but time, and their own puerile or wicked productions can

---

1. F 26:488–89; 1783.

show the inefficacy and dangerous tendency of. I think often of our situation and view it with concern. From the high ground we stood upon, from the plain path which invited our footsteps, to be so fallen! so lost! it is really mortifying; but virtue, I fear has, in a great degree, taken its departure from us; and the want of disposition to do justice is the source of the national embarrassments; for whatever guise or colorings are given to them, this I apprehend is the origin of the evils we now feel, and probably shall labor under for some time yet."[1]

JP: During that same time period, you repeatedly argued for a stronger central government. Were there any restrictions you thought should be placed on that federal government?

GW: Yes. I argued that "unless adequate powers are given to Congress for the *general* purposes of the federal union, . . . we shall soon molder into dust and become contemptible in the eyes of Europe." I added, "To suppose that the *general* concern of this country can be directed by thirteen heads, or one head without competent powers, is a solecism, the bad effects of which every man who has had the practical knowledge to judge from, that I have, is fully convinced of."[2]

JP: You had suffered under the tyranny of the British and then labored under the weakness of the Articles of Confederation. Under those circumstances, were you more concerned about a disjointed confederation or an overly strong central government?

GW: I predicted in 1784, "The disinclination of the individual states to yield competent powers to Congress for the federal government, their unreasonable jealousy of that body and of one another, and the disposition which seems to pervade each, of being all-wise and all-powerful within itself, will, if there is not a change in the system be our downfall as a nation. This is as

1. F 28:431; 1786.
2. F 27:49; 1783; emphasis added in second instance

clear to me as the A, B, C. . . . For my own part, although I am returned to, and am now mingled with the class of private citizens, and like them must suffer all the evils of a tyranny, or of too great an extension of federal powers; I have no fears arising from this source, in my mind, but I have many, and powerful ones indeed which predict the worst consequences from a half-starved, limping government, that appears to be always moving upon crutches, and tottering at every step."[1]

JP: Why were you not more concerned about the central government assuming too much power?

GW: I considered that "the rulers of [our] nation . . . are the creatures of our making, appointed for a limited and short duration, and who are amenable for every action, and recallable at any moment, and are subject to all the evils which they may be instrumental in producing."[2]

I noted my great fear: "I do not conceive we can exist long as a nation without having lodged somewhere a power, which will pervade the whole union in as energetic a manner, as the authority of the state governments extends over the several states."[3]

JP: What were some of the strengths you hoped the Constitution would have—as well as the restrictions that would be placed on it?

GW: I hoped that it would be "a liberal and energetic constitution, well guarded and closely watched, to prevent encroachments."[4]

Less than two months after the close of the Constitutional Convention, I expressed a concern to my nephew: "It is agreed on all hands that no government can be well administered without

---

1. F 27:305–7; 1784.
2. F 28:290; 1785.
3. F 28:502; 1786.
4. F 29:52; 1786.

powers; yet the instant these are delegated, although those who are entrusted with the administration are no more than the creatures of the people, act as it were but for a day, and are amenable for every false step they take, they are, from the moment they receive it, set down as tyrants; their natures, one would conceive from this, immediately changed, and that they could have no other disposition but to oppress. Of these things, in a government constituted and guarded as *ours* is, I have no idea; and do firmly believe that whilst many *ostensible* reasons are assigned to prevent the adoption of it, the real ones are concealed behind the curtain, because they are not of a nature to appear in open day. I believe further, supposing them pure, that as great evils result from too great jealousy as from the want of it. We need look I think no further for proof of this, than to the constitution of some if not all of these states. No man is a warmer advocate for proper restraints and wholesome checks in every department of government than I am; but I have never yet been able to discover the propriety of placing it absolutely out of the power of men to render essential services, because a possibility remains of their doing ill."[1]

JP: The Articles of Confederation had a weak Congress—and many feared strengthening it. But I understand you had a different view.

GW: Yes, I recall asking in a letter in 1783, "For heaven's sake, who are Congress? are they not the creatures of the people, amenable to them for their conduct, and dependent from day to day on their breath? Where then can be the danger of giving them such powers as are adequate to the great ends of government, and to all the general purposes of the Confederation (I repeat the word *general*, because I am no advocate for their having to do with the particular policy of any state, further than it concerns the union at large)."[2]

---

1. F 29:311–12; 1787.
2. F 27:51; 1783.

JP: What kind of powers did you feel Congress should have?

GW: "It is clearly my opinion, unless Congress have powers competent to all *general* purposes, that the distresses we have encountered, the expense we have incurred, and the blood we have spilt in the course of an eight years war, will avail us nothing."[1]

JP: Did you consider the judicial system to be an important part of the national government?

GW: "I have always been persuaded that the stability and success of the national government, and consequently the happiness of the people of the United States, would depend in a considerable degree on the interpretation and execution of its laws. In my opinion, therefore, it is important, that the judiciary system should not only be independent in its operations, but as perfect as possible in its formation."[2]

JP: Some have felt that the president, once elected, then has a mandate to do as he pleases. Do you agree with that view?

GW: No, my opinion and desire were stated thus: "I only wish, while I am a servant of the people, to know the will of my masters, that I may govern myself accordingly."[3]

JP: What was the attitude with which you sought to govern as president?

GW: "In every act of my administration, I have sought the happiness of my fellow-citizens. My system for the attainment of this object has uniformly been to overlook all personal, local and partial considerations: to contemplate the United States, as one great whole; . . . and to consult only the substantial and permanent interests of our country."[4]

---

1. F 26:188; 1783.
2. F 31:31; 1790.
3. F 33:96; 1793.
4. F 34:252; 1795.

"Though I shall always think it a sacred duty, to exercise with firmness and energy, the Constitutional powers with which I am vested, yet it appears to me no less consistent with the public good, than it is with my personal feelings, to mingle in the operations of government every degree of moderation and tenderness which the national justice, dignity and safety may permit."[1]

JP: In our day, we see much encroachment by one branch of government on another. Judges sometimes legislate from the bench. The president uses executive orders to create laws. The Congress constantly encroaches on the states. What do you say about this pattern?

GW: "It is important . . . that the habits of thinking in a free country should inspire caution in those entrusted with its administration, to confine themselves within their respective Constitutional spheres; avoiding in the exercise of the powers of one department to encroach upon another. The spirit of encroachment tends to consolidate the powers of all the departments in one, and thus to create, whatever the form of government, a real despotism. A just estimate of that love of power, and proneness to abuse it, which predominates in the human heart is sufficient to satisfy us of the truth of this position."[2]

JP: You were repeatedly disappointed in the lack of unity of the states.

GW: "We are either a united people, or we are not. If the former, let us, in all matters of general concern act as a nation, which have national objects to promote, and a national character to support. If we are not, let us no longer act a farce by pretending to it."[3]

---

1. F 34:390; 1795.
2. F 35:228; 1796.
3. F 28:336; 1785.

JP: How concerned were you that people or groups would seek to disrupt the union of the states?

GW: Right after the Revolutionary War, I said, "Whatever measures have a tendency to dissolve the union, or contribute to violate or lessen the sovereign authority, ought to be considered as hostile to the liberty and independency of America, and the authors of them treated accordingly."[1]

JP: What is the power of unity?

GW: "A hundred thousand men, coming one after another, cannot move a ton weight; but the united strength of fifty would transport it with ease."[2]

"While . . . every part of our country thus feels an immediate and particular interest in union, all the parts combined in the united mass of means and efforts cannot fail to find greater strength, greater resource, proportionally greater security from external danger, a less frequent interruption of their peace by foreign nations; and, what is of inestimable value! they must derive from union an exemption from those broils and wars between themselves, which so frequently afflict neighboring countries, not tied together by the same government; which their own rivalships alone would be sufficient to produce; but which opposite foreign alliances, attachments, and intrigues would stimulate and embitter."[3]

JP: It seems, then, that you feel the unity of our nation is absolutely vital.

GW: "The unity of government which constitutes you one people is also now dear to you. It is justly so; for it is a main pillar in the edifice of your real independence, the support of your tranquility at home; your peace abroad; of your safety; of

---

1. F 26:488; 1783.
2. F 27:51; 1783.
3. F 35:221; 1796.

your prosperity; of that very liberty which you so highly prize. But as it is easy to foresee that from different causes and from different quarters, much pains will be taken, many artifices employed, to weaken in your minds the conviction of this truth; as this is the point in your political fortress against which the batteries of internal and external enemies will be most constantly and actively (though often covertly and insidiously) directed, it is of infinite moment that you should properly estimate the immense value of your national union to your collective and individual happiness. . . .

"You should cherish a cordial, habitual and immoveable attachment to it; accustoming yourselves to think and speak of it as of the palladium of your political safety and prosperity; watching for its preservation with jealous anxiety; discountenancing whatever may suggest even a suspicion that it can in any event be abandoned, and indignantly frowning upon the first dawning of every attempt to alienate any portion of our country from the rest, or to enfeeble the sacred ties which now link together the various parts."[1]

JP: We are presently experiencing great disunity in our nation. What was your experience—and how did you feel about it?

GW: We were only three years into our new government when I lamented, "How unfortunate . . . that whilst we are encompassed on all sides with avowed enemies and insidious friends, that internal dissensions should be harrowing and tearing our vitals. . . . Without more charity for the opinions and acts of one another in governmental matters, or some more infallible criterion by which the truth of speculative opinions, before they have undergone the test of experience, are to be forejudged than has yet fallen to the lot of fallibility, I believe it will be difficult, if not impracticable, to manage the reins of government or to keep

---

1. F 35:218; 1796.

the parts of it together: for if, instead of laying our shoulders to the machine after measures are decided on, one pulls this way and another that, before the utility of the thing is fairly tried, it must, inevitably, be torn asunder. And, in my opinion the fairest prospect of happiness and prosperity that ever was presented to man, will be lost."[1]

JP: You felt that Americans should have greater loyalty to the United States than to their own individual state.

GW: "Citizens by birth or choice, of a common country, that country has a right to concentrate your affections. The name of *American,* which belongs to you, in your national capacity, must always exalt the just pride of patriotism, more than any appellation derived from local discriminations. With slight shades of difference, you have the same religion, manners, habits and political principles. You have in a common cause fought and triumphed together. The independence and liberty you possess are the work of joint councils, and joint efforts; of common dangers, sufferings and successes."[2]

---

1. F 32:310–31; 1792.
2. F 35:219; 1796.

George Washington, engraved by A. B. Durand,
from portrait by John Trumbull, 1792

5

Principles and Policies of Government

JP: Do you have any counsel for those who are creating a new government?

GW: I advised my brother John Augustine, when he and others were forming the state constitution of Virginia in 1776: "To form a new government, requires infinite care, and unbounded attention; for if the foundation is badly laid the superstructure must be bad, too. Much time therefore, [must] be bestowed in weighing and digesting matters well. . . . No time can be misspent that is employed in separating the wheat from the tares. . . . Every man should consider that he is lending his aid to frame a constitution which is to render millions happy, or miserable, and that a matter of such moment cannot be the work of a day."[1]

JP: James Madison wrote, "If men were angels, no government would be necessary. If angels were to govern men, neither external nor internal controls on government would be necessary. In framing a government which is to be administered by men over men, the great difficulty lies in this: you must first enable the government to control the governed; and in the next place oblige it to control itself."[2] Do you share that view?

---

1. F 5:92; 1776.
2. *Federalist*, no. 51.

GW: In discussing the government under the Articles of Confederation, I agreed: "We have probably had too good an opinion
of human nature in forming our confederation. Experience has
taught us that men will not adopt and carry into execution measures the best calculated for their own good, without the inter-
vention of a coercive power."[1]

JP: Why is that?

GW: Because too often we humans are basically selfish. "A
small knowledge of human nature will convince us that, with far
the greatest part of mankind, interest is the governing principle;
and that almost every man is more or less under its influence."[2]

A few years later I added, "It is not the public but the private
interest which influences the generality of mankind, nor can the
Americans any longer boast an exception."[3]

Unfortunately, "Mankind, when left to themselves, are unfit
for their own government."[4]

JP: What do you view as the ultimate object of government?

GW: "The aggregate happiness of the society, which is best
promoted by the practice of a virtuous policy, is, or ought to be,
the end of all government."[5]

JP: What did you identify as the foundation and pillars of our
government?

GW: "There are four things, which I humbly conceive, are essential to the well being, I may even venture to say, to the existence of the United States as an independent power:

---

1. F 28:502; 1786.
2. F 10:363; 1778.
3. F 24:421; 1782.
4. F 29:33–34; 1786.
5. F 31:142; 1790.

"1st. An indissoluble union of the states under one federal head.

"2dly. A sacred regard to public justice.

"3dly. The adoption of a proper peace establishment, and

"4thly. The prevalence of that pacific and friendly disposition, among the people of the United States, which will induce them to forget their local prejudices and policies, to make those mutual concessions which are requisite to the general prosperity, and in some instances, to sacrifice their individual advantages to the interest of the community.

"These are the pillars on which the glorious fabric of our independency and national character must be supported; liberty is the basis, and whoever would dare to sap the foundation, or overturn the structure, under whatever specious pretexts he may attempt it, will merit the bitterest execration, and the severest punishment which can be inflicted by his injured country."[1]

JP: With that foundation in place, what principles should good government adhere to?

GW: "As on one side, no local prejudices, or attachments; no separate views, nor party animosities, will misdirect the comprehensive and equal eye which ought to watch over this great assemblage of communities and interests: so, on another, that the foundations of our national policy will be laid in the pure and immutable principles of private morality; and the preeminence of a free government, be exemplified by all the attributes which can win the affections of its citizens, and command the respect of the world."[2]

JP: What is the best form of government?

GW: "Republicanism is not the phantom of a deluded imagination: on the contrary, . . . under no form of government, will

1. F 26:487; 1783.
2. F 30:294; 1789.

laws be better supported, liberty and property better secured, or happiness be more effectually dispensed to mankind."[1]

JP: A republican form of government seems to presuppose that the people are ultimately in charge.

GW: "The power under the Constitution will always be in the people. It is entrusted for certain defined purposes, and for a certain limited period, to representatives of their own choosing; and whenever it is executed contrary to their interest, or not agreeable to their wishes, their servants can, and undoubtedly will be, recalled."[2]

In my first inaugural address, I indicated my "fixed belief that this Constitution is really in its formation a government of the people; that is to say, a government in which all power is derived from, and at stated periods reverts to them—and that, in its operation, it is purely, a government of laws made and executed by the fair substitutes of the people alone."[3]

"It remains with the people themselves to preserve and promote the great advantages of their political and natural situation; nor ought a doubt to be entertained that men, who so well understand the value of social happiness, will ever cease to appreciate the blessings of a free, equal, and efficient government."[4]

JP: How much confidence did you have that the people would choose the right course?

GW: "The great mass of our citizens require only to understand matters rightly, to form right decisions."[5]

I was "persuaded that if ever a crisis should arise to call forth

---

1. F 34:99; 1795.
2. F 29:311; 1787.
3. F 30:299; 1789.
4. F 31:94n; 1790.
5. F 37:129; 1799.

the good sense and spirit of the people, no deficiency in either will be found."[1]

As I retired from the presidency, I reflected, "As for myself I am now seated in the shade of my vine and fig tree, and although I look with regret on many transactions which do not comport with my ideas, I shall, notwithstanding 'view them in the calm lights of mild philosophy,' persuaded, if any great crisis should occur, to require it, that the good sense and spirit of the major part of the people of this country, will direct them properly."[2]

JP: If the people's voice is to wield such great influence, they need to be heard.

GW: Yes. "Whatever my own opinion may be on this, or any other subject, interesting to the community at large, it always has been, and will continue to be, my earnest desire to learn, and to comply, as far as is consistent, with the public sentiment; but it is on *great* occasions *only*, and after time has been given for cool and deliberate reflection, that the *real* voice of the people can be known."[3]

After serving as president for most of two terms, I observed, "As it is the right of the people that [their will] should be carried into effect, their sentiments *ought* to be unequivocally known, that the principles on which the government has acted . . . may either be changed, or the opposition . . . may meet effectual discountenance."[4]

This is consistent with what I said near the beginning of my presidency: "It is desirable on all occasions, to unite with a steady and firm adherence to constitutional and necessary acts of government, the fullest evidence of a disposition, as far as may be practicable, to consult the wishes of every part of the community,

---

1. F 35:475; 1797.
2. F 35:471; 1797.
3. F 35:31; 1796.
4. F 35:453; 1797.

and to lay the foundations of the public administration in the affection of the people."[1]

JP: What are the limitations on listening to the voice of the people?

GW: One is lack of speed in bringing changes. "The people must *feel* before they will *see*, [and] consequently are brought slowly into measures of public utility."[2]

I expressed this a slightly different way in a letter to Lafayette: "Democratical states must always feel before they can see: it is this that makes their governments slow, but the people will be right at last."[3]

Another limitation is that "the wishes of the people, seldom founded in deep disquisitions, or resulting from other reasonings than their present feeling, may not entirely accord with our true policy and interest. If they do not, to observe a proper line of conduct, for promoting the one, and avoiding offense to the other, will be a work of great difficulty."[4]

"In a free and republican government, you cannot restrain the voice of the multitude; every man will speak as he thinks, or more properly without thinking, consequently will judge of effects without attending to the causes."[5]

Another circumstance in which to be hesitant is when the people are speaking as a mob: "The tumultuous populace of large cities are ever to be dreaded. Their indiscriminate violence prostrates for the time all public authority, and its consequences are sometimes extensive and terrible."[6]

JP: What about letting the minority's views hold sway?

1. F 31:400; 1791.
2. F 28:183; 1785.
3. F 28:208; 1785.
4. F 11:288; 1778.
5. F 12:383; 1778.
6. F 31:324; 1791.

GW: "If the minority, and a small one too, is suffered to dictate to the majority, after measures have undergone the most solemn discussions by the representatives of the people, and their will through this medium is enacted into a law, there can be no security for life, liberty, or property; nor, if the laws are not to govern, can any man know how to conduct himself in safety."[1]

Later I warned, "If the laws are to be . . . trampled upon, with impunity, and a minority . . . is to dictate to the majority, there is an end put, at one stroke, to republican government; and nothing but anarchy and confusion is to be expected thereafter."[2]

"To yield to the treasonable fury of [a] small . . . portion of the United States would be to violate the fundamental principle of our Constitution, which enjoins that the will of the majority shall prevail."[3]

In my Farewell Address, I noted a related concern about yielding to minorities: "All obstructions to the execution of the laws, all combinations and associations, under whatever plausible character, with the real design to direct, control, counteract, or awe the regular deliberation and action of the constituted authorities are destructive of this fundamental principle and of fatal tendency. They serve to organize faction, to give it an artificial and extraordinary force; to put in the place of the delegated will of the nation, the will of a party; often a small but artful and enterprising minority of the community; and, according to the alternate triumphs of different parties, to make the public administration the mirror of the ill concerted and incongruous projects of faction, rather than the organ of consistent and wholesome plans digested by common councils and modified by mutual interests.

"However combinations or associations of the above description may now and then answer popular ends, they are likely, in the course of time and things, to become potent engines, by

---

1. F 33:523; 1794.
2. F 33:465; 1794.
3. F 34:30; 1794.

which cunning, ambitious and unprincipled men will be enabled to subvert the power of the people, and to usurp for themselves the reins of government; destroying afterwards the very engines which have lifted them to unjust dominion."[1]

JP: Since the people are so crucial to good government, how important is it that they have freedom of speech?

GW: "If men are to be precluded from offering their sentiments on a matter, which may involve the most serious and alarming consequences that can invite the consideration of mankind, reason is of no use to us; the freedom of speech may be taken away, and, dumb and silent we may be led, like sheep, to the slaughter."[2]

JP: Is there a down side to freedom of the press?

GW: First, "If the government and the officers of it are to be the constant theme for newspaper abuse, and this too without condescending to investigate the motives or the facts, it will be impossible, I conceive, for any man living to manage the helm or to keep the machine together."[3]

Second, "It is well known that, when one side only of a story is heard and often repeated, the human mind becomes impressed with it insensibly."[4]

Third, "Serious misfortunes, originating in misrepresentation, frequently flow and spread before they can be dissipated by truth."[5]

JP: So how would you respond to lies or misrepresentations in the press?

---

1. F 35:224–25; 1796.
2. F 26:225; 1783.
3. F 32:137; 1792.
4. F 34:99; 1795.
5. F 35:37; 1796.

GW: "Those who are disposed to cavil, or who have the itch of writing strongly upon them, nothing can be made to suit their palates: the best way therefore to disconcert and defeat them is to take no notice of their publications; all else is but food for declamation."[1]

"Should anything present itself in this or any other publication [GW was addressing a man who planned a publication that was critical of Washington], I shall never undertake the painful task of recrimination, nor do I know that I should ever enter upon my justification."[2]

JP: Do you have any cautions for those who are pushing for change in government?

GW: "A spirit for political improvements seems to be rapidly and extensively spreading through the European countries. I shall rejoice in seeing the condition of the human race happier than ever it has hitherto been. But I should be sorry to see that those who are for prematurely accelerating those improvements were making *more haste than good speed* in their innovations. So much prudence, so much perseverance, so much disinterestedness and so much patriotism are necessary among the leaders of a nation, in order to promote the national felicity, that sometimes my fears nearly preponderate over my expectations."[3]

JP: What is your feeling about the extremes in government?

GW: "There is a natural and necessary progression, from the extreme of anarchy to the extreme of tyranny; and . . . arbitrary power is most easily established on the ruins of liberty abused to licentiousness."[4]

When I was president, I observed: "We are . . . anxious that . . .

---

1. F 28:327; 1785.
2. F 28:162; 1785.
3. F 31:40; 1790.
4. F 26:489; 1783.

the rights of man [be] so well understood and so permanently fixed, as while despotic oppression is avoided on the one hand, licentiousness may not be substituted for liberty nor confusion take place of order on the other. The just medium cannot be expected to be found in a moment, the first vibrations always go to the extremes, and cool reason, which can alone establish a permanent and equal government, is as little to be expected in the tumults of popular commotion, as an attention to the liberties of the people is to be found in the dark divan of a despotic tyrant."[1]

JP: Were you concerned about the enemies of the government?

GW: "The difference . . . between the friends, and foes of order, and good government, is . . . that, the latter are always working, like bees, to distil their poison; whilst the former, [depend] often times *too much,* and *too long* upon the sense, and good dispositions of the people."[2]

JP: You were also concerned about government being oppressive.

GW: "Government being, among other purposes, instituted to protect the persons and consciences of men from oppression, it certainly is the duty of rulers, not only to abstain from it themselves, but, according to their stations, to prevent it in others."[3]

JP: I'd like to ask a few questions about fiscal issues. Some in our time have tried to strengthen the economy by adding to the national debt. Do you feel that is good policy?

GW: As president, I repeatedly called for the elimination of the national debt:

1793: "I entertain a strong hope that the state of the national

---

1. F 32:54; 1792.
2. F 34:264; 1795.
3. F 30:416n; 1789.

finances is now sufficiently matured to enable you to enter upon a systematic and effectual arrangement for the regular redemption and discharge of the public debt, according to the right which has been reserved to the government. No measure can be more desirable, whether viewed with an eye to its intrinsic importance, or to the general sentiment and wish of the nation."[1]

"No pecuniary consideration is more urgent than the regular redemption and discharge of the public debt: on none can delay be more injurious, or an economy of time more valuable."[2]

1794: "The time, which has elapsed, since the commencement of our fiscal measures has developed our pecuniary resources, so as to open a way for a definitive plan for the redemption of the public debt. It is believed that the result is such as to encourage Congress to consummate this work, without delay. Nothing can more promote the permanent welfare of the nation, and nothing would be more grateful to our constituents. Indeed, whatsoever is unfinished of our system of public credit cannot be benefited by procrastination; and as far as may be practicable, we ought to place that credit on grounds which cannot be disturbed, and to prevent that progressive accumulation of debt which must ultimately endanger all governments."[3]

1796: "It will afford me heartfelt satisfaction to concur in such further measures as will ascertain to our country the prospect of a speedy extinguishment of the debt. Posterity may have cause to regret if, from any motive, intervals of tranquility are left unimproved for accelerating this valuable end."[4]

In my Farewell Address, I said plainly, "As a very important source of strength and security, cherish public credit. One method of preserving it is to use it as sparingly as possible: avoiding occasions of expense by cultivating peace, but remembering also that

---

1. F 32:211; 1793.
2. F 33:168; 1793.
3. F 34:36; 1794.
4. F 35:319; 1796.

timely disbursements to prepare for danger frequently prevent much greater disbursements to repel it; avoiding likewise the accumulation of debt, not only by shunning occasions of expense, but by vigorous exertions in time of peace to discharge the debts which unavoidable wars may have occasioned, not ungenerously throwing upon posterity the burden which we ourselves ought to bear. The execution of these maxims belongs to your representatives, but it is necessary that public opinion should cooperate."[1]

In the last year of my life I further observed, both as a matter of private and of public policy, that "to contract new debts is not the way to pay old ones."[2]

JP: In your Farewell Address you encouraged "shunning occasions of expense," which is one side of the governmental income-outgo equation. How did you feel about taxes?

GW: I added in that same address "that towards the payment of debts there must be revenue; that to have revenue there must be taxes; that no taxes can be devised which are not more or less inconvenient and unpleasant."[3]

JP: Certainly taxes are necessary. But is it appropriate for us to want to hold onto our own property?

GW: "It is . . . natural for man to wish to be the absolute lord and mastery of what he holds in occupancy."[4]

JP: As you consider dealing with economic inequities, would you ever be in favor of price controls?

GW: "To limit the prices of articles . . . I believe is inconsistent with the very nature of things and impracticable in itself."[5]

---

1. F 35:230; 1796.
2. F 37:177; 1799.
3. F 35:230; 1796.
4. F 35:500; 1797.
5. F 14:313; 1779.

JP: Let's talk about a few other topics. How vital is a nation's integrity?

GW: Here is where I stood: "Let us . . . as a nation be just," I said. "Let us fulfill the public contracts, which Congress had undoubtedly a right to make for the purpose of carrying on the war, with the same good faith we suppose ourselves bound to perform our private engagements."[1]

"I hold the maxim no less applicable to public than to private affairs, that honesty is always the best policy."[2]

JP: How important for our country is a good justice system?

GW: I wrote to U.S. Attorney General Edmund Randolph, "Impressed with a conviction that the due administration of justice is the firmest pillar of good government, I have considered the first arrangement of the judicial department as essential to the happiness of our country, and to the stability of its political system; hence the selection of the fittest characters to expound the law, and dispense justice, has been an invariable object of my anxious concern."[3]

Earlier, to Lafayette: "The best and only safe road to honor, glory, and true dignity is justice."[4]

JP: What should we do about laws we disagree with?

GW: "There never was a law yet made, I conceive, that hit the taste *exactly* of every man, or every part of the community; of course, if this be a reason for opposition, no law can be executed at all without force, and every man or set of men will in that case cut and carve for themselves; the consequences of which must be

---

1. F 26:489; 1783.
2. F 35:234; 1796.
3. F 30:418–19; 1789.
4. F 16:373; 1779.

deprecated by all classes of men, who are friends to order, and to the peace and happiness of the country."[1]

JP: What do you think of the practice of passing laws that we never intend to enforce?

GW: "Laws or ordinances unobserved, or partially attended to, had better never have been made; because the first is a mere nihil [nothing], and the second is productive of much jealousy and discontent."[2]

JP: What was your approach to the use of the veto? What about the line-item veto?

GW: As president, it was my practice to "give my signature to many bills with which my judgment is at variance. . . . From the nature of the Constitution, I must approve all parts of a bill, or reject it in total. To do the latter can only be justified upon the clear and obvious grounds of propriety; and I never had such confidence in my own faculty of judging as to be over tenacious of the opinions I may have imbibed in doubtful cases."[3]

JP: Immigration is currently a big issue in the United States. In your day, when the United States had vast, unsettled areas, were you in favor of fairly open immigration laws?

GW: "I had always hoped that this land might become a safe and agreeable asylum to the virtuous and persecuted part of mankind, to whatever nation they might belong."[4]

"The bosom of America is open to receive not only the opulent and respectable stranger, but the oppressed and persecuted of all nations and religions; whom we shall welcome to a participation

---

1. F 33:523–24; 1794.
2. F 29:191; 1787.
3. F 33:96; 1793.
4. F 29:504; 1788.

of all our rights and privileges, if by decency and propriety of conduct they appear to merit the enjoyment."[1]

"Let the poor the needy and oppressed of the earth, and those who want land, resort to the fertile plains of our western country, the second land of promise, and there dwell in peace, fulfilling the first and great commandment."[2]

JP: Did you feel immigrants could settle as discrete groups, or were you in favor of assimilation?

GW: "The policy or advantage of [immigration] taking place in a body (I mean the settling of them in a body) may be much questioned; for, by so doing, they retain the language, habits and principles (good or bad) which they bring with them. Whereas by an intermixture with our people, they, or their descendants, get assimilated to our customs, measures and laws: in a word, soon become one people."[3]

---

1. F 27:254; 1783.
2. F 28:203; 1785.
3. F 34:23; 1794.

George Washington, by Gilbert Stuart, about 1800 to 1820

6

Responsibilities of Citizens

JP: What is the role of citizen involvement in our nation? What will a good citizen do?

GW: As I concluded my service as president, I said, "No wish in my retirement can exceed that of seeing our country happy; and I can entertain no doubt of its being so, if all of us act the part of good citizens; contributing our best endeavors to maintain the Constitution, support the laws, and guard our independence against all assaults from whatsoever quarter they may come. Clouds may and doubtless often will, in the vicissitudes of events, hover over our political concerns, but a steady adherence to these principles will not only dispel them but render our prospects the brighter by such temporary obscurities."[1]

JP: Were you in favor of public service for American citizens?

GW: "I am clearly in sentiment with you that every man who is in the vigor of life ought to serve his country, in whatever line it requires and he is fit for."[2]

"It is not sufficient for a man to be a passive friend and well-wisher to the cause."[3]

---

1. F 35:423; 1797.
2. F 35:480; 1979.
3. F 4:450; 1776.

During the war I sent this message to Benedict Arnold: "Every post is honorable in which a man can serve his country."[1]

JP: You held the three highest offices a man could hold in your time: commander-in-chief of the army, president of the constitutional convention, and president of the United States. How did you view such elevated offices?

GW: "All see, and most admire, the glare which hovers round the external trappings of elevated office. To me there is nothing in it, beyond the luster which may be reflected from its connection with a power of promoting human felicity."[2]

JP: What was your overriding motivation in government service?

GW: The year of my death I said, "I have no object, separated from the general welfare, to promote. I have no predilections, no prejudices to gratify; no friends whose interests or views I wish to advance at the expense of propriety."[3]

Earlier in my service as president, I delineated my influences: "Next to a conscientious discharge of my public duties, to carry along with me the approbation of my constituents would be the highest gratification my mind is susceptible of; but, the latter being secondary, I cannot make the former yield to it."[4]

And still earlier: "To please everybody is impossible; were I to undertake it, I should probably please nobody. If I know myself I have no partialities. I have from the beginning, and I will to the end pursue to the best of my judgment and abilities one steady line of conduct for the good of the great whole. This will, un-

---

1. F 3:494; 1775.
2. F 30:496; 1790.
3. F 37:193; 1799.
4. F 34:311; 1795.

der all circumstances, administer consolation to myself, however short I may fall of the expectations of others."[1]

Even as early as 1756 I felt to write, "I have diligently sought the public welfare; and have endeavored to inculcate the same principles in all that are under me. These reflections will be a cordial to my mind as long as I am able to distinguish between good and evil."[2]

JP: Did you consider how your countrymen felt about you?

GW: "To stand well in the estimation of one's country is a happiness that no rational creature can be insensible of."[3]

JP: What counsel would you give to public officials?

GW: "In general I esteem it a good maxim, that the best way to preserve the confidence of the people durably is to promote their true interest."[4]

Further, "Men in responsible situations cannot, like those in private life, be governed *solely* by the dictates of their own inclinations, or by such motives as can only affect themselves. . . . A man in public office . . . is accountable for the consequences of his measures to others; and one in private life, who has no other check than the rectitude of his own actions."[5]

JP: You had a great deal of experience with legislators, including being one yourself. What advice would you give to those elected to legislative positions?

GW: "Speak seldom, but to important subjects, except such as particularly relate to your constituents, and, in the former case, make yourself perfectly master of the subject."[6]

---

1. F 15:97; 1779.
2. F 1:533; 1756.
3. F 16:8; 1779.
4. F 19:114; 1780.
5. F 35:167; 1796.
6. F 29:313; 1787.

JP: How necessary is it that we have close oversight of public officials?

GW: "However necessary it may be to keep a watchful eye over public servants and public measures, yet there ought to be limits to it; for suspicions unfounded, and jealousies too lively, are irritating to honest feeling; and oftentimes are productive of more evil than good."[1]

JP: What was your attitude toward impropriety among government officials?

GW: "The executive branch of this government never has, nor will suffer, while I preside, any improper conduct of its officers to escape with impunity."[2]

JP: Some politicians seem to act like they are infallible.

GW: Speaking of myself at the beginning of my service as president, I asked, "Shall I . . . set up my judgment as the standard of perfection? And shall I arrogantly pronounce that whosoever differs from me, must discern the subject through a distorting medium, or be influenced by some nefarious design? The mind is so formed in different persons as to contemplate the same object in different points of view. Hence originates the difference on questions of the greatest import, both human and divine. In all institutions of the former kind, great allowances are doubtless to be made for the fallibility and imperfection of their authors."[3]

Near the end of my service, I added, "If any power on earth could, or the great power above would, erect the standard of infallibility in political opinions, there is no being that inhabits this terrestrial globe that would resort to it with more eagerness than myself, so long as I remain a servant of the public. But as I have found no better guide hitherto than upright intentions and close

---

1. F 32:48; 1792.
2. F 34:402; 1795.
3. F 30:299; 1789.

investigation, I shall adhere to these maxims while I keep the watch; leaving it to those who will come after me to explore new ways, if they like; or think them better."[1]

It is true to say that I knew my own weaknesses: "It is only from the assurances of support, which I have received from the respectable and worthy characters in every part of the union, that I am enabled to overcome the diffidence which I have in my own abilities to execute my great and important trust to the best interest of your country. An honest zeal, and an unremitting attention to the interest of united America, is all that I dare promise."[2]

JP: It seems that people can't run for national office nowadays unless they are wealthy.

GW: "The compensations to the officers of the United States . . . appear to call for legislative revision. The consequences of a defective provision, are of serious import to the government. If private wealth is to supply the defect of public retribution, it will greatly contract the sphere within which the selection of characters for office is to be made, and will proportionally diminish the probability of a choice of men able, as well as upright. Besides that, it would be repugnant to the vital principles of our government virtually to exclude from public trusts, talents and virtue, unless accompanied by wealth."[3]

JP: What rules did you follow in making political appointments?

GW: Shortly before I was elected president, I observed, "Scarcely a day passes in which applications of one kind or another do not arrive. Insomuch that had I not early adopted some general principles, I should before this time have been wholly occupied in this business. . . . Should it be my lot to go again into

---

1. F 34:311; 1795.
2. F 30:317; 1789.
3. F 35:318; 1796.

public office, I would go into it, without being under any possible engagements of any nature whatsoever: that, so far as I know my own heart, I would not be in the remotest degree influenced, in making nominations, by motives arising from the ties of amity or blood: and that, on the other hand, three things, in my opinion, ought principally to be regarded, viz., the fitness of characters to fill offices, the comparative claims from the former merits and sufferings in service of the different candidates, and the distribution of appointments in as equal a proportion as might be to persons belonging to the different states in the union; for without precautions of this kind, I clearly foresaw the endless jealousies, and, possibly, the fatal consequences, to which a government, depending altogether on the good will of the people for its establishment, would certainly be exposed in its early stages."[1]

JP: Was one of those rules regarded as having greater weight than the others?
GW: "In every nomination to office I have endeavored, as far as my own knowledge extended, or information could be obtained, to make fitness of character my primary object."[2]

JP: Some people in high office make sure to surround themselves with their friends—or they want to reward their friends for their service.
GW: It was my strict rule that in making appointments, "esteem, love, and friendship [could] have no influence on my mind."[3]

JP: Some leaders seem to be most interested in rewarding their supporters.

1. F 30:238–39; 1789.
2. F 30:469; 1795.
3. F 36:461; 1798.

GW: I early resolved to "make it the most agreeable part of my duty to study merit, and reward the . . . deserving."[1]

JP: Did you have a personal policy about making political promises?

GW: "It is an invariable maxim with me, never, beforehand, and until the moment requires it, to pledge myself by promises which I might find embarrassing to comply with."[2]

JP: Since you were the first president, what was your approach to setting precedents?

GW: I noted that "the first transactions of a nation, like those of an individual upon his first entrance into life, make the deepest impression and are to form the leading traits in its character."[3]

Therefore, "as the first of everything, in our situation will serve to establish a precedent, it is devoutly wished on my part that these precedents may be fixed on true principles."[4]

And, "In our progress toward political happiness my station is new; and if I may use the expression, I walk on untrodden ground. There is scarcely any part of my conduct which may not hereafter be drawn into precedent."[5]

JP: Sometimes politicians neglect the long view and settle for temporary solutions.

GW: "I lament most sincerely, the system of policy which has been but too generally adopted in all the states, to wit, that of temporary expedients; which like quack medicines are so far from removing the causes of complaint that they only serve to increase the disorder."[6]

---

1. F 1:271; 1756.
2. F 36:383; 1798.
3. F 29:465; 1788.
4. F 30:210; 1789.
5. F 30:496; 1790.
6. F 22:282; 1781.

JP: Some leaders are very hesitant to ask their people to sacrifice. What is your view of asking for sacrifices in challenging times?

GW: "When any great object is in view, the popular mind is roused into expectation, and prepared to make sacrifices both of ease and property. If those, to whom they confide the management of their affairs, do not call them to make these sacrifices, and the object is not attained, or they are involved in the reproach of not having contributed as much as they ought to have done towards it, they will be mortified at the disappointment, they will feel the censure, and their resentment will rise against those, who, with sufficient authority, have omitted to do what their interest and their honor required."[1]

JP: You often spoke on how essential knowledge is to freedom.

GW: "Knowledge is in every country the surest basis of public happiness. In one in which the measures of government receive their impression so immediately from the sense of the community as in ours it is proportionally essential. To the security of a free Constitution it contributes in various ways: By convincing those who are entrusted with the public administration, that every valuable end of government is best answered by the enlightened confidence of the people: and by teaching the people themselves to know and to value their own rights; to discern and provide against invasions of them; to distinguish between oppression and the necessary exercise of lawful authority; between burdens proceeding from a disregard to their convenience and those resulting from the inevitable exigencies of society; to discriminate the spirit of liberty from that of licentiousness, cherishing the first, avoiding the last, and uniting a speedy, but temperate vigilance against encroachments, with an inviolable respect to the laws."[2]

---

1. F 19:114; 1780.
2. F 30:493; 1790.

JP: How important is it that citizens have a correct under-standing of current issues?

GW: "I am *sure* the mass of citizens in these United States *mean well*, and I firmly believe they will always *act well*, whenever they can obtain a right understanding of matters; but in some parts of the union, where the sentiments of their delegates and lead-ers are adverse to the government, and great pains are taken to inculcate a belief that their rights are assailed, and their liberties endangered, it is not easy to accomplish this; especially, as is the case invariably, when the inventors and abettors of pernicious measures use infinitely more industry in disseminating the poi-son, than the well-disposed part of the community to furnish the antidote. To this source all our discontents may be traced and from it our embarrassments proceed. Hence, serious misfortunes originating in misrepresentation frequently flow and spread be-fore they can be dissipated by truth."[1]

JP: You're famous for opposing political parties.

GW: "I was no party man myself, and the first wish of my heart was, if parties did exist, to reconcile them."[2]

Elsewhere I declared, "[I am] of no party, and [my] sole wish is to pursue, with undeviating steps, a path which would lead this country to respectability, wealth and happiness."[3]

JP: Why were you so opposed to political parties?

GW: Because of where they could lead. "If we mean to support the liberty and independence which it has cost us so much blood and treasure to establish, we must drive far away the demon of party spirit and local reproach."[4]

"Much indeed to be regretted, party disputes are now carried

---

1. F 35:37; 1796.
2. F 35:119; 1796.
3. F 34:251; 1795.
4. F 31:48; 1790.

to such a length, and truth is so enveloped in mist and false representation, that it is extremely difficult to know through what channel to seek it. . . . But such . . . is the turbulence of human passions in party disputes, when victory more than truth is the palm contended for."[1]

"The common and continual mischiefs of the spirit of party are sufficient to make it the interest and duty of a wise people to discourage and restrain it."[2]

One of my most detailed objections to parties is found in my Farewell Address: "Let me . . . warn you in the most solemn manner against the baneful effects of the spirit of party. . . .

"This spirit, unfortunately, is inseparable from our nature, having its root in the strongest passions of the human mind. It exists under different shapes in all governments, more or less stifled, controlled, or repressed; but, in those of the popular form it is seen in its greatest rankness and is truly their worst enemy. . . .

"It serves always to distract the public councils and enfeeble the public administration. It . . . kindles the animosity of one part against another. . . .

"There is an opinion that parties in free countries are useful checks upon the administration of the government and serve to keep alive the spirit of liberty. This within certain limits is probably true. . . . But in those of the popular character, in governments purely elective, it is a spirit not to be encouraged. From their natural tendency, it is certain there will always be enough of that spirit for every salutary purpose. And there being constant danger of excess, the effort ought to be, by force of public opinion, to mitigate and assuage it. A fire not to be quenched; it demands a uniform vigilance to prevent its bursting into a flame, lest instead of warming it should consume."[3]

---

1. F 34:251; 1795.
2. F 35:227; 1796.
3. F 35:226; 1796.

JP: What would you say to those who choose party over principle?

GW: "It is . . . most devoutly to be wished that faction [were] at an end and that those to whom everything dear and valuable is entrusted would lay aside party views and return to first principles. Happy, happy, thrice happy country if such was the government of it, but alas! we are not to expect that the path is to be strewed with flowers. That great and good Being who rules the universe has disposed matters otherwise and for wise purposes, I am persuaded."[1]

"If principles, instead of men, are not the steady pursuit of [a party], their cause will soon be at an end."[2]

JP: What should we do about the extreme partisan views that are being advanced nowadays?

GW: "Differences in political opinions are as unavoidable as, to a certain point, they may, perhaps, be necessary; but it is exceedingly to be regretted that subjects cannot be discussed with temper on the one hand, or decisions submitted to without having the motives which led to them improperly implicated on the other: and this regret borders on chagrin when we find that men of abilities, zealous patriots, having the same *general* objects in view, and the same upright intentions to prosecute them, will not exercise more charity in deciding on the opinions and actions of one another. When matters get to such lengths, the natural inference is that both sides have strained the cords beyond their bearing, and that a middle course would be found the best, until experience shall have decided on the right way, or, which is not to be expected, because it is denied to mortals, there shall be some infallible rule by which we could *forejudge* events."[3]

---

1. F 13:348; 1778.
2. F 37:349; 1799.
3. F 32:132; 1792.

JP: What was your approach to dealing with differences of opinion?

GW: "My friendship is not in the least lessened by the difference, which has taken place in our political sentiments. . . . Men's minds are as variant as their faces, and, where the motives to their actions are pure, the operation of the former is no more to be imputed to them as a crime, than the appearance of the latter; for both, being the work of nature, are equally unavoidable. Liberality and charity, instead of clamor and misrepresentation (which later only serve to foment the passions, without enlightening the understanding), ought to govern in all disputes."[1]

"The mind is so formed in different persons as to contemplate the same object in different points of view. Hence originates the difference on questions of the greatest import, both human and divine. In all institutions of the former kind, great allowances are doubtless to be made for the fallibility and imperfection of their authors."[2]

"A difference of opinion on political points is not to be imputed to freemen as a fault since it is to be presumed that they are all actuated by an equally laudable and sacred regard for the liberties of their country. If the mind is so formed in different persons as to consider the same object to be somewhat different in its nature and consequences as it happens to be placed in different points of view, . . . we ought, indeed, rather to rejoice that so much has been effected than to regret that more could not all at once be accomplished."[3]

When Thomas Jefferson and Alexander Hamilton were unable to agree, I expressed my feelings to Jefferson, saying: "I will frankly and solemnly declare that I believe the views of both of you are pure and well meant; and that experience alone will decide with respect to the salubrity of the measures which are

---

1. F 30:223; 1789.
2. F 30:299; 1789.
3. F 30:347n; 1789.

the subjects of dispute. Why then, when some of the best citizens in the United States, men of discernment, uniform and tried patriots, who have no sinister views to promote but are chaste in their ways of thinking and acting are to be found, some on one side, and some on the other of the questions which have caused these agitations, should either of you be so tenacious of your opinions as to make no allowances for those of the other? . . . I have a great, a sincere esteem and regard for you both, and ardently wish that some line could be marked out by which both of you could walk."[1]

Besides, "the views of men can only be known, or guessed at, by their words or actions."[2]

JP: As a leader, what was your approach to dealing with disputes?

GW: "To constitute a dispute there must be two parties. To understand it well, both parties and all the circumstances must be fully heard, and to accommodate differences, temper and mutual forbearance are requisite."[3]

JP: You were one of the greatest leaders of all time. What counsel on leadership would you give others?

GW: "Require nothing unreasonable of your officers and men, but see that whatever is required be punctually complied with. Reward and punish every man according to his merit, without partiality or prejudice; hear his complaints; if well founded, redress them; if otherwise, discourage them, in order to prevent frivolous ones. Discourage vice in every shape, and impress upon the mind of every man, from the first to the lowest, the importance of the cause and what it is they are contending for."[4]

---

1. F 32:185; 1792.
2. F 37:89; 1799.
3. F 31:29; 1790.
4. F 4:80; 1775.

And have effective follow through: "Orders, unless they are followed by close attention to the performance of them, are of little avail."[1]

Finally, "The true distinction   between what is called a fine regiment, and an indifferent one, will ever, upon investigation, be found to originate in and depend upon the care, or the inattention, of the officers belonging to them."[2]

JP: We seem to have a pattern of leaders who appear to hide or twist the truth.

GW: "Candor is not a more conspicuous trait in the character of governments than it is of individuals."[3]

JP: Some leaders lean on their office or title to give them authority.

GW: "Remember that it is the *actions*, and not the commission, that make the officer, and that there is more expected from him, than the *title*."[4]

"Diffidence in an officer is a good mark because he will always endeavor to bring himself up to what he conceives to be the full line of his duty."[5]

JP: And what about the power of example?

GW: "Example, whether it be good or bad, has a powerful influence, and the higher in rank the officer is, who sets it, the more striking it is."[6]

JP: Since we're talking about the duties of citizens, how important is it that we be a virtuous and moral people?

---

1. F 18:71; 1780.
2. F 26:68; 1783.
3. F 36:18; 1797.
4. F 1:271; 1756.
5. F 7:471; 1777.
6. F 18:72; 1780.

GW: "Without virtue and without integrity, the finest talents of the most brilliant accomplishments can never gain the respect or conciliate the esteem of the truly valuable part of mankind."[1]

JP: You often connected our happiness with the need for morality and virtue.

GW: "There is no truth more thoroughly established than that there exists in the economy and course of nature an indissoluble union between virtue and happiness; between duty and advantage; between the genuine maxims of an honest and magnanimous policy, and the solid rewards of public prosperity and felicity; since we ought to be no less persuaded that the propitious smiles of Heaven can never be expected on a nation that disregards the eternal rules of order and right, which Heaven itself has ordained."[2]

"A good general government, without good morals and good habits, will not make us a happy people; and we shall deceive ourselves if we think it will."[3]

"Purity of morals [is] the only sure foundation of public happiness in any country."[4]

"While I reiterate the professions of my dependence upon Heaven as the source of all public and private blessings; I will observe that the general prevalence of piety; philanthropy, honesty, industry, and economy seems, in the ordinary course of human affairs, particularly necessary for advancing and conforming the happiness of our country. While all men within our territories are protected in worshipping the Deity according to the dictates of their consciences, it is rationally to be expected from them in return, that they will be emulous of evincing the sanctity of their professions by the innocence of their lives and the beneficence of

---

1. F 35:422; 1797.
2. F 30:294; 1789.
3. F 30:76; 1788.
4. F 13:118; 1778.

their actions; for no man, who is profligate in his morals or a bad member of the civil community, can possibly be a true Christian or a credit to his own religious society."[1]

"Can it be that Providence has not connected the permanent felicity of a nation with its virtue? The experiment, at least, is recommended by every sentiment which ennobles human nature."[2]

---

1. F 30:336; 1789.
2. F 35:231; 1796.

George Washington, by Rembrandt Peale, about 1795 to 1823

7

War, Peace, and International Relations

JP: Is there value in the study of the art of war?

GW: "The art of war is at once comprehensive and complicated;
. . . it demands much previous study; and . . . the possession of
it, in its most improved and perfect state, is always a great moment to the security of a nation. This, therefore, ought to be a
serious care of every government; and for this purpose, an acad-
emy, where a regular course of instruction is given, is an obvious
expedient, which different nations have successfully employed."[1]

JP: Is it ever appropriate for a nation to take the offensive in
war—or should we simply be defensive?

GW: "Offensive operations oftentimes are the surest, if not the
only (in some cases), means of defense."[2]

"It has been very properly the policy of our government to
cultivate peace. But in contemplating the possibility of our being driven to unqualified war, it will be wise to anticipate that
frequently the most effectual way to defend is to attack."[3]

JP: What are the limits on retaliation in war?

GW: "Retaliation is certainly just and sometimes necessary,

---

1. F 35:317; 1796.
2. F 37:50; 1799.
3. F 37:37; 1798.

even where attended with the severest penalties; but when the evils which may and must result from it exceed those intended to be redressed, prudence and policy require that it should be avoided."[1]

JP: How vital is it that our nation have a strong defense?

GW: "My primary objects, and to which I have steadily adhered, have been to preserve the country in peace if I can, and to be prepared for war if I cannot. [And] to effect the first upon terms consistent with the respect which is due to ourselves, and with honor, justice and good faith to all the world."[2]

"Although we cannot, by the best concerted plans, absolutely command success, although, the race is not always to the swift, or the battle to the strong, yet without presumptuously waiting for miracles to be wrought in our favor, it is our *indispensable duty*— with the deepest gratitude to Heaven for the past, and humble confidence in its smiles on our future operations—to make use of all the means in our power for our defense and security."[3]

"We shall never have peace till the enemy are convinced that we are in a condition to carry on the war. It is no new maxim in politics that for a nation to obtain peace, or insure it, it must be prepared for war."[4]

"If we are wise, let us prepare for the worst; there is nothing which will so soon produce a speedy and honorable peace as a state of preparation for war."[5]

JP: How important is it that we have experienced soldiers in our military?

GW: "To expect . . . the same service from raw and undisci-

---

1. F 7:211; 1777.
2. F 33:414; 1794.
3. F 23:478; 1782.
4. F 19:133; 1780.
5. F 25:151; 1782.

plined recruits, as from veteran soldiers, is to expect what never did and perhaps never will happen. Men who are familiarized to danger meet it without shrinking, whereas those who have never seen service often apprehend danger where no danger is."[1]

JP: How did you feel about the establishment and use of militias?

GW: "It may be laid down as a primary position, and the basis of our system, that every citizen who enjoys the protection of a free government, owes not only a proportion of his property, but even his personal services to the defense of it, and consequently that the citizens of America (with a few legal and official exceptions), from eighteen to fifty years of age, should be borne on the militia rolls, provided with uniform arms, and so far accustomed to the use of them that the total strength of the country might be called forth at a short notice on any very interesting emergency."[2]

JP: What do you think of patriotism as a motivator in war?

GW: "Men may speculate as they will; they may talk of patriotism; they may draw a few examples from ancient story, of great achievements performed by its influence; but whoever builds upon it, as a sufficient basis for conducting a long and [bloody] war, will find themselves deceived in the end. We must take the passions of men as nature has given them, and those principles as a guide which are generally the rule of action. I do not mean to exclude altogether the idea of patriotism. I know it exists, and I know it has done much in the present contest. But I will venture to assert that a great and lasting war can never be supported on this principle alone. It must be aided by a prospect of interest or some reward. For a time, it may, of itself push men to action;

---

1. F 4:316; 1776.
2. F 26:389; 1783.

to bear much, to encounter difficulties; but it will not endure unassisted by interest."[1]

JP: Does patriotism have a down side?
GW: We must "guard against the impostures of pretended patriotism."[2]

JP: Even though you first became known to Americans as a man of war, it is clear that you much preferred peace.
GW: "How pitiful, in the eye of reason and religion, is that false ambition which desolates the world with fire and sword for the purposes of conquest and fame; when compared to the milder virtues of making our neighbors and our fellow men as happy as their frail conditions and perishable natures will permit them to be."[3]

"My first wish is to see this plague to mankind banished from off the earth, and the sons and daughters of this world employed in more pleasing and innocent amusements, than in preparing implements and exercising them for the destruction of mankind."[4]

"The friends of humanity will deprecate war, wheresoever it may appear; and we have experienced enough of its evils in this country to know that it should not be wantonly or unnecessarily entered upon. I trust, therefore, that the good citizens of the United States will show to the world that they have as much wisdom in preserving peace . . . as they have heretofore displayed valor in defending their just rights."[5]

"For the sake of humanity, it is devoutly to be wished that the manly employment of agriculture and the humanizing benefits

---

1. F 11:286; 1778.
2. F 35:236; 1796.
3. F 30:5; 1788.
4. F 28:202; 1785.
5. F 32:460; 1793.

of commerce would supersede the waste of war and the rage of conquest; and the swords might be turned into ploughshares, the spears into pruning-hooks, and as the Scripture expresses it, 'the nations learn war no more.'"[1]

JP: Are there times when we should not seek peace?

GW: "To discerning men, nothing can be more evident, than that a peace on the principles of dependence, however limited, after what has happened, would be to the last degree dishonorable and ruinous."[2]

JP: What is the best way to ensure peace in troubled times?

GW: "The United States ought not to indulge a persuasion that, contrary to the order of human events, they will forever keep at a distance those painful appeals to arms, with which the history of every other nation abounds. There is a rank due to the United States among nations, which will be withheld, if not absolutely lost, by the reputation of weakness. If we desire to avoid insult, we must be able to repel it; if we desire to secure peace, one of the most powerful instruments of our rising prosperity, it must be known that we are at all times ready for war."[3]

As I noted a moment ago, "To be prepared for war is one of the most effectual means of preserving peace."[4]

JP: What about ongoing enmity among nations?

GW: "Nothing is more essential, than that permanent, inveterate antipathies against particular nations, and passionate attachments for others, should be excluded; and that, in place of them, just and amicable feelings towards all should be cultivated. The nation, which indulges towards another an habitual hatred, or

---

1. F 29:485; 1788.
2. F 11:289; 1778.
3. F 33:165–66; 1793.
4. F 30:491; 1790.

an habitual fondness, is in some degree a slave. It is a slave to its animosity or to its affection, either of which is sufficient to lead it astray from its duty and its interest. Antipathy in one nation against another disposes each more readily to offer insult and injury, to lay hold of slight causes of umbrage, and to be haughty and intractable, when accidental or trifling occasions of dispute occur. Hence frequent collisions, obstinate, envenomed, and bloody contests."[1]

JP: Let's talk about foreign relations. Do you have a basic caution when it comes to foreign relations?

GW: "Our own experience (if it has not already had this effect) will soon convince us that *disinterested* favors, or friendship from any nation whatever, is too novel to be calculated on; and there will always be found a wide difference between the words and actions of any of them."[2]

"It is a maxim, founded on the universal experience of mankind, that no nation is to be trusted farther than it is bound by its interest; and no prudent statesman or politician will venture to depart from it."[3]

JP: What was your attitude about forming alliances with other nations?

GW: "My policy has been, and will continue to be, while I have the honor to remain in the administration of the government, to be upon friendly terms with, but independent of, all the nations of the earth. To share in the broils of none. To fulfill our own engagements. To supply the wants, and be carriers for them all: being thoroughly convinced that it is our policy and interest to do so."[4]

---

1. F 35:231; 1796.
2. F 35:449; 1797.
3. F 13:256; 1778.
4. F 34:401; 1795.

To put it another way, "I hope the United States of America will be able to keep disengaged from the labyrinth of European politics and wars. . . . It should be the policy of united America to administer to their wants, without being engaged in their quarrels. And it is not in the ability of the proudest and most potent people on earth to prevent us from becoming a great, a respectable and a commercial nation, if we shall continue united and faithful to ourselves."[1]

In my Farewell Address I declared, "'Tis our true policy to steer clear of permanent alliances, with any portion of the foreign world. So far, I mean, as we are now at liberty to do it, for let me not be understood as capable of patronizing infidelity to existing engagements. . . . But in my opinion, it is unnecessary and would be unwise to extend them. Taking care always to keep ourselves, by suitable establishments, on a respectably defensive posture, we may safely trust to temporary alliances for extraordinary emergencies."[2]

JP: How did you feel about the United States being involved in the affairs of nations across the Atlantic?

GW: "Separated as we are by a world of water from other nations, if we are wise we shall surely avoid being drawn into the labyrinth of their politics and involved in their destructive wars."[3]

JP: So you felt we should simply be independent of other nations.

GW: "My ardent desire is, and my aim has been (as far as depended upon the executive department,) to comply strictly with *all* our engagements, foreign and domestic; but to keep the United States free from *political* connections with *every* other coun-

---

1. F 30:71; 1788.
2. F 35:234; 1796.
3. F 29:406; 1788.

try. To see that they *may be* independent of *all*, and under the influence of *none*. In a word, I want an *American* character, that the
powers of Europe may be convinced we act for *ourselves* and not
for *others*; this in my judgment, is the only way to be respected
abroad and happy at home and not by becoming the partisans
of Great Britain or France, create dissensions, disturb the public
tranquility, and destroy, perhaps forever the cement which binds
the union."[1]

JP: Do you think the United States should be involved in so-
called nation building?
GW: "I wish well to all nations and to all men. My politics
are plain and simple. I think every nation has a right to establish
that form of government under which it conceives it shall live
most happy; provided it infracts no right or is not dangerous
to others. And that no governments ought to interfere with the
internal concerns of another, except for the security of what is
due to themselves."[2]

JP: Do you have fears about foreign influence?
GW: "Against the insidious wiles of foreign influence, . . . the
jealousy of a free people ought to be *constantly* awake; since history and experience prove that foreign influence is one of the
most baneful foes of republican government. But that jealousy to
be useful must be impartial; else it becomes the instrument of the
very influence to be avoided, instead of a defense against it."[3]

JP: Some feel that the United States should operate more under international law. What is your view?
GW: "If we are to be told by a foreign power . . . what we shall

---

1. F 34:335; 1795.
2. F 37:70; 1798.
3. F 35:233; 1796.

do, and what we shall not do, we have independence yet to seek, and have contended hitherto for very little."[1]

But "we are an independent nation, and act for ourselves. Having fulfilled, and being willing to fulfill, (as far as we are able) our engagements with other nations, and having decided on, and strictly observed a neutral conduct towards the belligerent powers, from an unwillingness to involve ourselves in war. We will not be dictated to by the politics of any nation under heaven, farther than treaties require of us."[2]

JP: What is the best policy toward foreign trade?

GW: "The great rule of conduct for us, in regard to foreign nations is in extending our commercial relations to have with them as little *political* connection as possible. So far as we have already formed engagements let them be fulfilled, with perfect good faith. Here let us stop."[3]

"Harmony [and] liberal intercourse with all nations, are recommended by policy, humanity and interest. But even our commercial policy should hold an equal and impartial hand: neither seeking nor granting exclusive favors or preferences; consulting the natural course of things; diffusing and diversifying by gentle means the streams of commerce, but forcing nothing, establishing with powers so disposed; in order to give to trade a stable course, to define the rights of our merchants, and to enable the government to support them; conventional rules of intercourse, the best that present circumstances and mutual opinion will permit, but temporary, and liable to be from time to time abandoned or varied, as experience and circumstances shall dictate; constantly keeping in view that 'tis folly in one nation to look for disinterested favors from another; that it must pay with a portion of its independence for whatever it may accept under that character;

---

1. F 35:40; 1796.
2. F 35:40; 1796.
3. F 35:233; 1796.

that by such acceptance, it may place itself in the condition of having given equivalents for nominal favors and yet of being reproached with ingratitude for not giving more. There can be no greater error than to expect, or calculate upon real favors from nation to nation. 'Tis an illusion which experience must cure, which a just pride ought to discard."[1]

JP: Do you believe in favoritism toward some nations to the exclusion of others?

GW: "Observe good faith and justice towards all nations; cultivate peace and harmony with all. Religion and morality enjoin this conduct; and can it be that good policy does not equally enjoin it? It will be worthy of a free, enlightened, and, at no distant period, a great nation, to give to mankind the magnanimous and too novel example of a people always guided by an exalted justice and benevolence."[2]

---

1. F 35:235; 1796.
2. F 35:231; 1796.

The Prayer at Valley Forge, by Henry Brueckner, 1866

8

Religion and God

JP: It is common for many in our nation today to think it is neither needful nor appropriate to be dependent on God. How do you feel about this kind of thinking?

GW: "It is the duty of all nations to acknowledge the providence of Almighty God, to obey his will, to be grateful for his benefits, and humbly to implore his protection and favor."[1]

JP: You felt that God had a purpose for you and America.

GW: "As it has been a kind of destiny that has thrown me upon this service, I shall hope that my undertaking it is designed to answer some good purpose. . . . I shall rely, therefore, confidently on that Providence, which has heretofore preserved and been bountiful to me."[2]

"When I contemplate the interposition of Providence, as it was visibly manifested in guiding us through the revolution, in preparing us for the reception of the general government, and in conciliating the good-will of the people of America toward one another after its adoption, I feel myself oppressed and almost overwhelmed with a sense of divine munificence. I feel that nothing is due to my personal agency in all those wonderful and

---

1. F 30:427; 1789.
2. F 3:294; 1775.

complicated events, except what can be attributed to an honest zeal for the good of my country."[1]

JP: Do you believe that God was involved in the establishment of America?

GW: I feel it deeply, and I said so often. Here is a small sampling of the things I said about this over the years:

To Governor Jonathan Trumbull of Connecticut, 1775: "The cause of our common country calls us both to an active and dangerous duty; divine Providence, which wisely orders the affairs of men, will enable us to discharge it with fidelity and success."[2]

General Orders, 1776: "Thursday the seventh instant, being set apart by the honorable the legislature of this province, as a day of fasting, prayer, and humiliation, to implore the Lord, and Giver of all victory, to pardon our manifold sins and wickedness's, and that it would please him to bless the continental arms, with his divine favor and protection'—All officers, and soldiers, are strictly enjoined to pay all due reverence, and attention on that day, to the sacred duties due to the Lord of hosts, for his mercies already received, and for those blessings, which our holiness and uprightness of life can alone encourage us to hope through his mercy to obtain."[3]

To John Washington, 1776: "It is to be hoped that, if our cause is just, as I do most religiously believe it to be, the same Providence which in many instances appeared for us, will still go on to afford its aid."[4]

General Orders, 1776: "We have . . . to resolve to conquer or to die. Our own, our country's honor, calls upon us for a vigorous and manly exertion; and if we now shameful fail, we shall become infamous to the whole world. Let us then rely on the goodness of our cause, and the aid of the Supreme Being, in whose hands victory is, to animate and encourage us to great and noble actions. The eyes of all our countrymen are now upon us, and we shall have their

---

1. Sparks, 12:145; 1789.
2. F 3:344; 1775.
3. F 4:369; 1776.
4. F 5:93; 1776.

blessings and praises, if happily we are the instruments of saving them from the tyranny mediated against them."[1]

To Edmund Pendleton, 1777: "That the God of Armies may enable me to bring the present contest to a speedy and happy conclusion, thereby gratifying me in a retirement to the calm and sweet enjoyment of domestic happiness, is the fervent prayer, and most ardent wish of my Soul."[2]

To Major General Israel Putnam, 1777: "Should providence be pleased to crown our arms in the course of the campaign, with one more fortunate stroke, I think we shall have no great cause for anxiety respecting the future designs of Britain. I trust all will be well in his good time."[3]

To Landon Carter, 1778: "My friends therefore may believe me sincere in my professions of attachment to them, whilst Providence has a joint claim to my humble and grateful thanks, for its protection and direction of me, through the many difficult and intricate scenes, which this contest hath produced; and for the constant interposition in our behalf, when the clouds were heaviest and seemed ready to burst upon us. To paint the distresses and perilous situation of this army in the course of last winter, for want of clothes, provisions, and almost every other necessary, essential to the well-being, I may say existence, of an army, would require more time and an abler pen than mine; nor, since our prospects have so miraculously brightened, shall I attempt it, or even bear it in remembrance, further than as a memento of what is due to the great Author of all the care and good that have been extended in relieving us in difficulties and distress."[4]

To Brigadier General Thomas Nelson, 1778: "The hand of Providence has been so conspicuous in all this that he must be worse than an infidel that lacks faith, and more wicked that has not gratitude to acknowledge his obligations; but it will be time enough for me to turn preacher when my present appointment ceases; and therefore, I shall add no more on the doctrine of Providence."[5]

General Orders, 1778: "It having pleased the Almighty ruler of the

---

1. F 5:211; 1776.
2. F 7:394; 1777.
3. F 9:400; 1777.
4. F 11:492; 1778.
5. F 12:343; 1778.

universe propitiously to defend the cause of the United American-States and finally by raising us up a powerful friend among the princes of the earth to establish our liberty and independence up lasting foundations, it becomes us to set apart a day for gratefully acknowledging the divine goodness and celebrating the important event which we owe to his benign interposition."[1]

General Orders, 1781: "The commander-in-chief earnestly recommends that the troops not on duty should universally attend with that seriousness of deportment and gratitude of heart which the recognition of such reiterated and astonishing interposition of Providence demands of us."[2]

To Thomas McKean, 1781: "I take a particular pleasure in acknowledging that the interposing Hand of Heaven, in the various instances of our extensive preparation for this operation (Yorktown), has been most conspicuous and remarkable."[3]

General Orders announcing the end of the war, 1783: "The commander in chief orders the cessation of hostilities between the United States of America and the king of Great Britain to be publicly proclaimed tomorrow at 12 o'clock at the new building, and that the Proclamation which will be communicated herewith, be read tomorrow evening at the head of every regiment and corps of the army. After which the chaplains with the several brigades will render thanks to almighty God for all his mercies, particularly for his over ruling the wrath of man to his own glory, and causing the rage of war to cease amongst the nations."[4]

To the Reverend John Rodgers, 1783: "I accept, with much pleasure your kind congratulations on the happy event of peace, with the establishment of our liberties and independence. Glorious indeed has been our contest: glorious in its issue; but in the midst of our joys, I hope we shall not forget that, to divine providence is to be ascribed the glory and the praise."[5]

General Orders, 1780: "Treason of the blackest dye was yesterday discovered! General Arnold who commanded at West Point, lost to

---

1. F 11:354; 1778.
2. F 23:247; 1781.
3. F 23:343; 1781.
4. F 26:334; 1783.
5. F 27:1; 1783.

every sentiment of honor, of public and private obligation, was about to deliver up that important post into the hands of the enemy. Such an event must have given the American cause a deadly wound if not fatal stab. Happily the treason had been timely discovered to prevent the fatal misfortune. The providential train of circumstances which led to it affords the most convincing proof that the liberties of America are the object of divine protection."[1]

To John Laurens, 1780: "In no instance since the commencement of the war, has the interposition of Providence appeared more remarkably conspicuous than in the rescue of the post and garrison of West Point from Arnold's villainous perfidy."[2]

To William Gordon, 1781: "We have, as you very justly observe, abundant reason to thank Providence for its many favorable interpositions in our behalf. It has at times been my only dependence, for all other resources seemed to have failed us."[3]

To the New Jersey legislature, 1783: "For me, it is enough to have seen the divine Arm visibly outstretched for our deliverance, and to have received the approbation of my country, and my conscience."[4]

To the militia officers of Philadelphia, 1783: "While the various scenes of the war, in which I have experienced the timely aid of the militia of Philadelphia, recur to my mind, my ardent prayer ascends to Heaven that they may long enjoy the blessings of that peace which has been obtained by the divine benediction on our common exertions."[5]

To Benjamin Lincoln, 1788: "I trust in that Providence, which has saved us in six troubles yea in seven, to rescue us again from any imminent, though unseen, dangers. Nothing, however, on our part ought to be left undone."[6]

To Annis Boudinot Stockton, 1788: "I can never trace the concatenation of causes, which led to these events, without acknowledging the mystery and admiring the goodness of Providence. To that su-

1. F 20:95; 1780.
2. F 20:173; 1780.
3. F 21:332; 1781.
4. F 27:261; 1783.
5. F 27:266; 1783.
6. F 30:63; 1788.

perintending Power alone is our retraction from the brink of ruin to be attributed."[1]

To the Hebrew congregations of Savannah, Georgia, 1789: "May the same wonder-working Deity, who long since delivered the Hebrews from their Egyptian oppressors, planted them in a promised land, whose providential agency has lately been conspicuous in establishing these United States as an independent nation, still continue to water them with the dews of heaven and make the inhabitants of every denomination participate in the temporal and spiritual blessings of that people whose God is Jehovah."[2]

To the citizens of Baltimore, 1789: "I know the delicate nature of the duties incident to the part which I am called to perform [serving as president], and I feel my incompetence, without the singular assistance of Providence, to discharge them in a satisfactory manner. But having undertaken the task from a sense of duty, no fear of encountering difficulties, and no dread of losing popularity, shall ever deter me from pursuing what I conceive to be the true interests of my country."[3]

To the German Reformed congregations, 1789: "I am happy in concurring with you in the sentiments of gratitude and piety towards Almighty God, which are expressed with such fervency of devotion in your address."[4]

To the Hebrew congregation of Newport, Rhode Island, 1790: "May the father of all mercies scatter light, and not darkness, upon our paths, and make us in all our several vocations useful here, and in His own due time and way everlastingly happy."[5]

To the Marquis de Lafayette, 1791: "We must, however, place a confidence in that Providence who rules great events, trusting that out of confusion he will produce order, and, notwithstanding the dark clouds, which may threaten at present, that right will ultimately be established."[6]

---

1. F 30:76; 1788.
2. Sparks, 12:186; 1789.
3. F 30:288; 1789.
4. Sparks, 12:156; 1789.
5. Schultz, 286; 1790.
6. F 31:324; 1791.

To John Armstrong, 1792: "I am sure that never was a people, who had more reason to acknowledge a Divine interposition in their affairs, than those of the United States; and I should be pained to believe that they have forgotten that agency, which was so often manifested during our Revolution, or that they failed to consider the omnipotence of that God who is alone able to protect them."[1]

Sixth annual address, 1794: "Let us unite, therefore, in imploring the Supreme Ruler of nations, to spread his holy protection over these United States; to turn the machinations of the wicked to the confirming of our constitutions; to enable us at all times to root out internal sedition, and put invasion to flight; to perpetuate to our country that prosperity, which his goodness has already conferred, and to verify the anticipation of this government being a safeguard to human rights."[2]

Eighth annual message to Congress, 1796: "The situation in which I now stand, for the last time, in the midst of the representatives of the people of the United States, naturally recalls the period when the administration of the present form of government commenced; and I cannot omit the occasion, to congratulate you and my country, on the success of the experiment; nor to repeat my fervent supplications to the Supreme Ruler of the Universe, and Sovereign Arbiter of Nations, that his Providential care may still be extended to the United States; that the virtue and happiness of the people, may be preserved; and that the government, which they have instituted, for the protection of their liberties, may be perpetual."[3]

To John Adams, 1797: "Although guided by our excellent Constitution in the discharge of official duties, and actuated, through the whole course of my public life, solely by a wish to promote the best interests of our country; yet, without the beneficial interposition of the Supreme Ruler of the Universe, we could not have reached the distinguished situation which we have attained with such unprecedented rapidity. To HIM, therefore, should we bow with gratitude and reverence, and endeavor to merit a continuance of HIS special favors."[4]

---

1. F 32:2; 1792.
2. F 34:37; 1794.
3. F 35:319–20; 1796.
4. F 35:431; 1797.

To John Adams, 1798: "Satisfied, therefore, that you have sincerely wished and endeavored to avert war, and exhausted to the last drop, the cup of reconciliation, we can with pure hearts appeal to Heaven for the justice of our cause, and may confidently trust the final result to that kind Providence who has heretofore, and so often, signally favored the people of these United States."[1]

JP: It's clear you believe that God has an interest in the success of America.

GW: A few years after the Revolutionary War, when things were still very much unsettled, I expressed, in clear understatement, my conviction that "the foundation of a great empire is laid, and I please myself with a persuasion that Providence will not leave its work imperfect."[2]

JP: While we are talking about God, I must say that in our day it has become commonplace to use His name in common speech, in irreverent and profane ways. What is your feeling about that?

GW: In General Orders I observed to the troops that "many and pointed orders have been issued against that unmeaning and abominable custom of swearing, not withstanding which, with much regret the General observes that it prevails, if possible, more than ever; his feelings are continually wounded by the oaths and imprecations of the soldiers whenever he is in hearing of them. The name of that Being, from whose bountiful goodness we are permitted to exist and enjoy the comforts of life is incessantly imprecated and profaned in a manner as wanton as it is shocking. For the sake therefore of religion, decency and order, the General hopes and trusts that officers of every rank will use their influence and authority to check a vice, which is as unprofitable as it is wicked and shameful. If officers would make it an invariable rule to reprimand, and if that does not do punish

---

1. F 36:328–29; 1798.
2. F 28:501; 1786.

soldiers for offences of this kind it could not fail of having the desired effect."[1]

JP: In your view, what is the role of religion and morality in politics and life?

GW: In my Farewell Address I said without equivocation, "Of all the dispositions and habits which lead to political prosperity, religion and morality are indispensable supports. In vain would that man claim the tribute of patriotism who should labor to subvert these great pillars of human happiness, these firmest props of the duties of man and citizens. The mere politician, equally with the pious man, ought to respect and to cherish them. A volume could not trace all their connections with private and public felicity. Let it simply be asked, Where is the security for property, for reputation, for life, if the sense of religious obligation desert the oaths, which are the instruments of investigation in courts of justice? And let us with caution indulge the supposition that morality can be maintained without religion. Whatever may be conceded to the influence of refined education on minds of peculiar structure, reason and experience both forbid us to expect that national morality can prevail in exclusion of religious principle. It is substantially true that virtue or morality is a necessary spring of popular government. The rule, indeed, extends with more or less force to every species of free government. Who, that is a sincere friend to it, can look with indifference upon attempts to shake the foundation of the fabric?"[2]

JP: What is the interrelationship between government and religion?

GW: "While just government protects all their religious rights, true religion affords to government its surest support."[3]

---

1. F 16:13; 1779.
2. F 35:229; 1796.
3. F 30:432n; 1789.

JP: Do you feel that religious freedom is an important part of the U.S. Constitution?

GW: Absolutely. In a speech to representatives of the United Baptist Churches of Virginia I assured them, "If I could have entertained the slightest apprehension that the Constitution framed by the convention where I had the honor to preside might possibly endanger the religious rights of any ecclesiastical society certainly I would never have placed my signature to it: and if I could now conceive that the general government might ever be so administered as to render the liberty of conscience insecure, I beg you will be persuaded that no one would be more zealous than myself to establish effectual barriers against the horrors of spiritual tyranny and every species of religious persecution."[1]

Two weeks later I addressed a letter to the Methodist Episcopal Church wherein I stated, "It shall still be my endeavor to manifest, by overt acts, the purity of my inclination for promoting the happiness of mankind, as well as the sincerity of my desires to contribute whatever may be in my power towards the preservation of the civil and religious liberties of the American people."[2]

Later that year I said to the Presbyterians, "It will be your care to instruct the ignorant, and to reclaim the devious, and, in the progress of morality and science, to which our government will give every furtherance, we may confidently expect the advancement of true religion, and the completion of our happiness."[3]

And still later I wrote a letter to the members of the New Church in Baltimore that "we have abundant reason to rejoice that in this land the light of truth and reason has triumphed over the power of bigotry and superstition, and that every person may here worship God according to the dictates of his own heart. In this enlightened age and in this land of equal liberty it is our boast that a man's religious tenets will not forfeit the protection

---

1. F 30:321n; 1789.
2. Federer, 653; 1789.
3. F 30:453n; 1789.

of the laws, nor deprive him of the right of attaining and holding the highest offices that are known in the United States."[1]

JP: What is your view of religious freedom?

GW: "I have often expressed my sentiments that every man, conducting himself as a good citizen, and being accountable to God alone for his religious opinions, ought to be protected in worshipping the Deity according to the dictates of his own conscience."[2]

But not only that. In 1789 I added: "The liberty enjoyed by the people of these states of worshiping Almighty God agreeably to their conscience is not only among the choicest of their blessings, but also of their rights. While men perform their social duties faithfully, they do all that society or the state can with propriety demand or expect; and remain responsible only to their Maker for the religion or modes of faith which they may prefer or profess."[3]

JP: Did you feel that Sunday worship services were beneficial?

GW: I spoke plainly to my troops, "The Commander in Chief thinks it a duty to declare the regularity and decorum with which divine service is now performed every Sunday, will reflect great credit on the army in general, tend to improve the morals, and at the same time, to increase the happiness of the soldiery, and must afford the most pure and rational entertainment for every serious and well-disposed mind."[4]

Not only that, but I said, "Divine service is to be performed tomorrow in the several brigades or divisions. The Commander in Chief earnestly recommends that the troops not on duty should universally attend with that seriousness of deportment and grat-

---

1. F 32:315; 1793.
2. F 30:321n; 1789.
3. F 30:416n; 1789.
4. F 26:250; 1783.

itude of heart which the recognition of such reiterated and astonishing interpositions of Providence demand of us."[1]

JP: But how do you feel about the religious conflict we continue to have?

GW: It troubles me. I wrote to a general convention of bishops
of the Protestant Episcopal Church: "It would ill become me to
conceal the joy I have felt in perceiving the fraternal affection,
which appears to increase every day among the friends of genuine religion. It affords edifying prospects indeed, to see Christians of different denominations, dwell together in more charity
and conduct themselves in respect to each other, with a more
Christian-like spirit than ever they have done in any former age,
or in any other nation."[2]

JP: What did you make of the contentiousness about religion
among your fellowman?

GW: In one letter I bemoaned the fact that "of all the animosities which have existed among mankind, those which are caused
by difference of sentiments in religion appear to be the most
inveterate and distressing, and ought most to be deprecated. I
was in hopes that the enlightened and liberal policy, which has
marked the present age, would at least have reconciled Christians of every denomination so far that we should never again
see the religious disputes carried to such a pitch as to endanger
the peace of society."[3]

JP: How did you feel to react when things in your life didn't
seem to work out?

GW: "At disappointments and losses which are the effects of
Providential acts, I never repine; because I am sure the all-wise

---

1. F 23:247; 1781.
2. Sparks, 12:162; 1789.
3. F 32:190; 1792.

disposer of events knows better than we do, what is best for us, or what we deserve."[1]

"I look upon every dispensation of Providence as designed to answer some valuable purpose, and hope I shall always possess a sufficient degree of fortitude to bear without murmuring any stroke which may happen, either to my person or estate, from that quarter."[2]

"The determinations of Providence are all ways wise; often inscrutable, and though its decrees appear to bear hard upon us at times is nevertheless meant for gracious purposes."[3]

JP: So you feel we should submit ourselves to God's will?

GW: When a friend lost a daughter in 1773, I tried to encourage him by saying, "The ways of Providence being inscrutable, and the justice of it not to be scanned by the shallow eye of humanity, nor to be counteracted by the utmost efforts of human power or wisdom, resignation, and as far as the strength of our reason and religion can carry us, a cheerful acquiescence to the Divine will, is what we are to aim."[4]

Twenty years later I felt the same way: "The will of Heaven is not to be controverted or scrutinized by the children of this world. It therefore becomes the creatures of it to submit with patience and resignation to the will of the Creator whether it be to prolong, or to shorten the number of our days. To bless them with health, or afflict them with pain."[5]

JP: If we put ourselves in the hands of God, can we just trust him to make everything work out right?

1. F 33:375; 1794.
2. F 15:180; 1779.
3. F 11:3; 1778.
4. F 3:133; 1773.
5. F 32:315; 1793.

GW: "To trust altogether in the justice of our cause, without our own utmost exertions, would be tempting Providence."[1]

JP: How did you view the involvement of God in your life?

GW: "I am . . . grateful to that Providence which has directed my steps, and shielded me in the various changes and chances, through which I have passed, from my youth to the present moment."[2]

JP: It sounds, then, that you did not see God as a Being who was distant from the needs and wants of mankind.

GW: I referred to Him as "that great and glorious Being, . . . [who] is the beneficent Author of all the good that was, that is, or that will be."[3]

JP: Were there times when felt you were personally protected by God?

GW: There were a number of times. For example, in a letter I sent to my brother after a battle in 1755, I credited God with my survival: "By the all-powerful dispensations of Providence, I have been protected beyond all human probability and expectation; for I had four bullets through my coat, and two horses shot under me, yet escaped unhurt, although death was leveling my companions on every side."[4]

In my final address to the nation, I said with all my heart, "I consider it an indispensable duty to close this last solemn act of my official life, by commending the Interests of our dearest country to the protection of Almighty God, and those who have the superintendence of them, to his holy keeping."[5]

---

1. F 5:390; 1776.
2. F 36:49; 1797.
3. F 30:427; 1789.
4. F 1:152; 1755.
5. F 27:285; 1783.

JP: Would it be correct, then, to say that you felt God had a direct influence on your life?

GW: "If such talents as I possess have been called into action by great events, and those events have terminated happily for our country, the glory should be ascribed to the manifest interposition of an overruling Providence."[1]

He was the source of all my blessings. I told Martha in 1775 that "I go [to war] fully trusting in that Providence, which has been more bountiful to me than I deserve."[2]

JP: Were you a prayerful man?

GW: It was part of who I was. I often prayed for my safety and that of my wife. When Martha was still my fiancée, in 1758, I assured her, "Since that happy hour when we made our pledges to each other, my thoughts have been continually going to you as another self. That an all-powerful Providence may keep us both in safety is the prayer of your ever faithful and affectionate friend."[3]

I also asked the army to pray: "The General most earnestly requires and expects . . . of all officers and soldiers not engaged in actual duty, a punctual attendance of Divine services, to implore the blessing of Heaven upon the means used for our safety and defense."[4]

I wrote in 1783: "For my own part, gentlemen, in whatever situation I shall be hereafter, my supplications, will ever ascend to Heaven, for the prosperity of my country in general; and for the individual happiness of those who are attached to the freedom, and independence of America."[5]

In my first inaugural address, in 1789, I emphasized: "It would be peculiarly improper to omit in this first official act my fervent

---

1. Sparks, 12:167; 1789.
2. F 3:301; 1775.
3. F 2:242; 1758.
4. F 3:309; 1775.
5. F 27:252–53; 1783.

supplications to that Almighty Being who rules over the universe, who presides in the councils of nations, and whose providential aids can supply every human defect, that his benediction may consecrate to the liberties and happiness of the people of the United States, a government instituted by themselves for these essential purposes: and may enable every instrument employed in its administration to execute with success, the functions allotted to his charge. In tendering this homage to the Great Author of every public and private good, I assure myself that it expresses your sentiments not less than my own; nor those of my fellow-citizens at large, less than either. No people can be bound to acknowledge and adore the invisible hand, which conducts the affairs of men more than the people of the United States. Every step, by which they have advanced to the character of an independent nation, seems to have been distinguished by some token of providential agency."[1]

This was part of a lifelong pattern. When I was twenty years old, I recorded this prayer in a manuscript book: "O Most Glorious God, in Jesus Christ, my merciful and loving Father; I acknowledge and confess my guilt in the weak and imperfect performance of the duties of this day. . . . I humbly beseech Thee to be merciful to me in the free pardon of my sins for the sake of Thy dear Son and only Savior Jesus Christ who came to call not the righteous, but sinners to repentance. Thou gavest Thy Son to die for me. Make me to know what is acceptable in Thy sight, and therein to delight, open the eyes of my understanding, and help me thoroughly to examine myself concerning my knowledge, faith, and repentance, increase my faith, and direct me to the true object, Jesus Christ the Way, the Truth, and the Life."[2]

JP: Did you feel that it was important that those who were laboring in the same cause should pray?

---

1. F 30:294; 1789.
2. Johnson, 24–35; 1752.

GW: In 1776 my message to the army was, "The Continental Congress having ordered, Friday the 17th instant to be observed as a day of 'fasting, humiliation and prayer, humbly to supplicate the mercy of Almighty God, that it would please him to pardon all our manifold sins and transgressions, and to prosper the arms of the united colonies, and finally, establish the peace and freedom of America, upon a solid and lasting foundation'— The General commands all officers, and soldiers, to pay strict obedience to the orders of the Continental Congress, and by their unfeigned, and pious observance of their religious duties, incline the Lord, and Giver of Victory, to prosper our arms."[1]

JP: Did you feel that the prayers of others helped you?

GW: I told a group of Methodist bishops in 1789, "I take in the kindest part the promise you make of presenting your prayers at the Throne of Grace for me, and that I likewise implore the divine benedictions on yourselves and your religious community."[2]

JP: Do you feel we are independent of God as individuals?

GW: Of course not! In 1778 I insisted to the Reverend Israel Evans, "It will ever be the first wish of my heart to aid your pious endeavors to inculcate a due sense of the dependence we ought to place in that all wise and powerful Being on whom alone our success depends."[3]

Further, I believe that "there is a Destiny which has the control of our actions, not to be resisted by the strongest efforts of human nature."[4]

Finally, I believe that "God alone is the judge of the hearts of men, and to him only in this case, they are answerable."[5]

---

1. F 5:43; 1776.
2. Sparks, 12:154; 1789.
3. F 11:78; 1778.
4. F 2:288; 1758.
5. F 3:492; 1775.

JP: Some historians today like to claim that you did not believe in Jesus Christ as our Savior.

GW: In general orders in 1779 I wholeheartedly quoted a congressional proclamation that said clearly, speaking of God, "He hath diffused the glorious light of the gospel, whereby, through the merits of our gracious Redeemer; we may become the heirs of His eternal glory." I then recommended that the states appoint "a day of public and solemn thanksgiving to Almighty God for the continuance of his favor and protection to these United States; . . . that he would in mercy look down upon us, pardon our sins and receive us into his favor."[1]

On another occasion I acknowledged Jesus Christ as "the Divine Author of our blessed religion" and said that we could never be a "happy nation" without following his example: "I now make it my earnest prayer that God would have you, and the state over which you preside, in his holy protection, that he would incline the hearts of the citizens to cultivate a spirit of subordination and obedience to government, to entertain a brotherly affection and love for one another, for their fellow citizens of the United States at large, and particularly for their brethren who have served in the field, and finally, that he would most graciously be pleased to dispose us all, to do justice, to love mercy, and to demean ourselves with that charity, humility and pacific temper of mind, which were the characteristics of the Divine Author of our blessed religion, and without an humble imitation of whose example in these things, we can never hope to be a happy nation."[2]

In a speech to the Delaware Indians in 1779, I said, "You do well to wish to learn our arts and ways of life, and above all, the religion of Jesus Christ. These will make you a greater and happier people than you are."[3]

1. F 17:190; 1779.
2. F 26:496; 1783.
3. F 15:55; 1779.

I repeatedly emphasized to the army that they should follow Christ in their lives. For instance, in general orders in 1778 I wrote: "While we are zealously performing the duties of good citizens and soldiers, we certainly ought not to be inattentive to the higher duties of religion. To the distinguished character of patriot, it should be our highest glory to add the more distinguished character of Christian. The signal instances of Providential goodness which we have experienced and which have now almost crowned our labors with complete success demand from us in a peculiar manner the warmest returns of gratitude and piety to the Supreme Author of all good."[1]

Some desired to send Christian missionaries to the Indians. I called it a "laudable and arduous an undertaking," and referred to it as "an event so long and so earnestly desired."[2]

JP: Did you believe in a Creator?

GW: I was convinced that "the task of studying the works of the great Creator [is] inexpressibly delightful."[3]

And I spoke of "fulfilling those obligations which are enjoined by your Creator and due to his creatures [as] highly pleasing and satisfactory to me."[4]

JP: Were you a church-going man?

GW: I wrote to the United Episcopal Churches of Christ Church and St. Peter's, "It is with peculiar satisfaction I can say that, prompted by a high sense of duty in my attendance on public worship, I have been gratified, during my residence among you, by the liberal and interesting discourses which have been delivered in your churches."[5]

---

1. F 11:342; 1778.
2. F 29:489; 1788.
3. F 27:270; 1783.
4. F 35:294–95; 1796.
5. F 35:410; 1797.

JP: What kinds of prayers were you taught at church?

GW: In terms of formal prayers, as an Anglican, I prayed from the Book of Common Prayer. These, of course, are not my own words, but the General Confession of the Morning Prayer went as follows: "Almighty and most merciful Father; we have erred, and strayed from thy ways like lost sheep. We have followed too much the devices and desires of our own hearts. We have offended against thy holy laws. We have left undone those things which we ought to have done; and we have done those things which we ought not to have done; and there is no health in us. But thou, O Lord, have mercy upon us, miserable offenders. Spare thou them, O God, who confess their faults. Restore thou those who are penitent; according to thy promises declared unto mankind in Christ Jesus our Lord. And grant, O most merciful Father, for his sake; that we may hereafter live a godly, righteous, and sober life, to the glory of thy holy Name. Amen."[1]

JP: I understand you repeatedly stood as a sponsor or god-father for a child being baptized. Do you recall the questions you were required to answer?

GW: Typically the priest would ask: "Dost thou believe in God the Father Almighty, Maker of heaven and earth? And in Jesus Christ his only-begotten Son our Lord? And that he was conceived by the Holy Ghost; born of the Virgin Mary; that he suffered under Pontius Pilate, was crucified, dead, and buried; that he went down into hell, and also did rise again the third day; that he ascended into heaven, and sitteth at the right hand of God the Father Almighty; and from thence shall come again at the end of the world, to judge the quick and the dead? And dost thou believe in the Holy Ghost; the holy Catholic Church; the communion of saints; the remission of sins; the resurrection of the flesh; and everlasting life after death?"

---

1. Lillback, 617.

Then, according to the pattern, the sponsor would answer, "All this I steadfastly believe."[1]

JP: What was your feeling about life after death?

GW: When I informed my nephew Burwell Bassett about the death of my stepdaughter, I expressed my faith in these words: "It is an easier matter to conceive, than to describe the distress of this family; especially that of the unhappy parent of our dear Patsy Custis, when I inform you that yesterday removed the sweet innocent girl entered into a more happy and peaceful abode than any she has met with in the afflicted path she hitherto has trod."[2]

A quarter of a century later, when I learned of the death of my brother Charles, I shared my feeling that "the death of near relations always produces awful and affecting emotions, under whatsoever circumstances it may happen. . . . When I shall be called upon to follow them, is known only to the Giver of Life. When the summons comes I shall endeavor to obey it with good grace."[3]

When my own mother died in 1789, I commiserated with my sister, Elizabeth Lewis, saying, "Awful and affecting as the death of a parent is, there is consolation in knowing that heaven has spared ours to an age beyond which few attain, and favored her with the full enjoyment of her mental faculties, and as much bodily strength as usually falls to the lot of four score. Under these considerations, and a hope that she is translated to a happier place, it is the duty of her relatives to yield due submission to the decrees of the Creator."[4]

JP: What was your attitude toward preparing for death?

---

1. Lillback, 617.
2. F 3:138; 1773.
3. F 37:372; 1799.
4. F 30:399; 1789.

GW: "Life is always uncertain, and common prudence dictates to every man the necessity of settling his temporal concerns, while it is in his power, and while the mind is calm and undisturbed."[1]

---

1. F 3:294–95; 1775.

Washington's Family, by Edward Savage, between 1789 and 1796

9

Relations with Others

JP: Let's talk about our relations with others. What is the best measure of true friendship?

GW: "A slender acquaintance with the world must convince every man that actions, not words are the true criterion of the attachment of his friends, and that the most liberal professions of good-will are very far from being the surest marks of it. I should be happy that my own experience had afforded fewer examples of the little dependence to be placed on them."[1]

I also advised: "Be courteous to all, but intimate with few; and let those few be well tried before you give them your confidence. True friendship is a plant of slow growth, and must undergo and withstand the shocks of adversity before it is entitled to the appellation."[2]

And: "Select the most deserving only for your friendships, and before this becomes intimate, weigh their dispositions and character well. True friendship is a plant of slow growth; to be sincere, there must be a congeniality of temper and pursuits. Virtue and vice cannot be allied; nor can idleness and industry."[3]

---

1. F 17:266; 1779.
2. F 26:39–40; 1783.
3. F 35:295; 1796.

JP: Would you pretend to be friends with someone else just to get along?

GW: "The arts of dissimulation . . . I despise, and my feelings will not permit me to make professions of friendship to the man I deem my enemy, and whose system of conduct forbids it."[1]

JP: What counsel would you give in regard to our associations with others?

GW: First, I copied this from *Rules of Civility:* "Associate with men of good quality, if you esteem your own reputation; for it is better to be alone than in bad company."[2]

Second, "Good company will always be found much less expensive than bad."[3]

Third, "It is easy to make acquaintances, but very difficult to shake them off, however irksome and unprofitable they are found, after we have once committed ourselves to them."[4]

Fourth, "It is at all times more easy to make enemies than friends."[5]

Fifth: "The most certain way to make a man your enemy is to tell him you esteem him such."[6]

JP: Even though you tried to strictly live by correct principles, you still made enemies.

GW: "It is a tax, however, severe, which all those must pay, who are called to eminent stations of trust, not only to be held up as conspicuous marks to the enmity of the public adversaries to their country, but to the malice of secret traitors and the *envious intrigues* of false friends and factions."[7]

---

1. F 10:249; 1778.
2. Rules of Civility #56; 1745.
3. F 30:247; 1789.
4. F 26:39; 1783.
5. F 35:295; 1796.
6. F 11:291; 1778.
7. F 10:415; 1778.

Further, "Against the malignancy of the discontented, the turbulent, and the vicious, no abilities, no exertions, nor the most unshaken integrity are any safeguard."[1]

JP: How did you feel about the individual citizens of an enemy nation?

GW: "I was opposed to the policy of [Great Britain] and became an enemy to her measures; but I always distinguished between a cause and individuals; and while the latter supported their opinions upon liberal and generous grounds, personally, I never could be an enemy to them."[2]

JP: You always seemed to be a good judge of others. How did you do it?

GW: "However it may be the practice of the world . . . to consider *that* only as meritorious which is attended with success, I have accustomed myself to judge of human actions very differently, and to appreciate them, by the manner in which they are conducted, more than by the *events*; which, it is not in the power of human foresight or prudence to command."[3]

JP: So you're saying that since we can't always control outcomes, we need to allow for how people conducted themselves—is that correct?

GW: Yes, and also "a man's *intentions* should be allowed in some respects to plead for his actions."[4]

JP: How did you view the errors you may have made in your public service?

GW: I asked the good people of the nation, "If the enlightened

---

1. F 34:16; 1794.
2. F 27:56; 1783.
3. F 25:415; 1782.
4. F 1:532; 1756.

and virtuous part of the community will make allowances for my involuntary errors, I will promise they shall have no cause to accuse me of willful ones."[1]

JP: And what did you say about the errors of others?

GW: "A man may err once, and he may err twice but when those who possess more than a common share of abilities persevere in a regular course of destructive policy, one is more apt to suspect their hearts than their heads."[2]

Later, in regard to excuses, I said, "It is better to offer no excuse than a bad one if at any time you should happen to fall into error."[3]

JP: What about being critical of errors in the past?

GW: "To rectify past blunders is impossible, but we might profit by the experience of them."[4]

Because of that, "We ought not to look back, unless it is to derive useful lessons from past errors, and for the purpose of profiting by dear-bought experience. To inveigh against things that are past and irremediable, is unpleasing; but to steer clear of the shelves and rocks we have struck upon, is the part of wisdom, equally as incumbent on political as other men."[5]

JP: Some people will try to excuse themselves because others also have erred.

GW: "I shall never attempt to palliate my own faults by exposing those of another."[6]

JP: What is the best way to deal with mistakes?

---

1. F 34:447; 1796.
2. F 22:283; 1781.
3. F 31:408; 1791.
4. F 19:133; 1780.
5. F 21:378; 1781.
6. F 16:151; 1779.

GW: "It is much easier at all times to prevent an evil than to rectify mistakes."[1]

JP: What is your observation about people who feel unjustly treated?

GW: "Nothing is too extravagant to expect from men who conceive they are ungratefully and unjustly dealt by, especially too if ... characters are wanting, to foment every passion which leads to discord."[2]

JP: What kept you going when others were criticizing your every move?

GW: One thing was to know that criticism always comes on those in prominent positions. "Why should I expect to be exempt from censure, the unfailing lot of an elevated station? Merits and talents with which I can have no pretensions of rivalship have ever been subject to it."[3]

"For myself, I expected not to be exempted from obloquy any more than others. It is the lot of humanity. But if the shafts of malice had been aimed at me in ever so pointed a manner ... , shielded as I was by a consciousness of having acted in conformity to what I believed my duty, they would have fallen blunted from their mark."[4]

JP: What was your reaction to censure?

GW: At one point during my presidency, I asked, "In what will this abuse terminate? The result, as it respects myself, I care not; for I have a consolation within that no earthly efforts can deprive me of, and that is that neither ambitious nor interested motives have influenced my conduct. The arrows of malevolence,

---

1. F 36:403; 1798.
2. F 26:234; 1783.
3. F 10:411; 1778.
4. F 30:42; 1788.

therefore, however barbed and well pointed, never can reach the most vulnerable part of me; though, whilst I am *up* as a *mark*, they will be continually aimed."[1]

Three years later, I said, "I am attacked for a steady opposition to every measure which has a tendency to disturb the peace and tranquility of [the country]. But these attacks, unjust and unpleasant as they are, will occasion no change in my conduct; nor will they work any other effect in my mind, than to increase the anxious desire which has long possessed my breast, to enjoy in the shades of retirement the consolation of having rendered my country every service my abilities were competent to, uninfluenced by pecuniary or ambitious considerations as they respected myself, and without any attempt to provide for my friends farther than their merits, abstractedly, entitle them to; nor an attempt in *any* instance to bring a relation of mine into office. Malignity therefore may dart her shafts; but no earthly power can deprive me of the consolation of knowing that I have not in the course of my administration been guilty of a *willful* error, however numerous they may have been from other causes."[2]

I added in 1797: "For the divisions which have taken place among us, with respect to our political concerns; for the attacks which have been made upon those to whom the administration of the government hath been entrusted *by the people*; and for the calumnies which are leveled at all those who are disposed to support the measures thereof, I feel, on public account, as much as any man can do; because (in my opinion) much evil, and no good can result from such conduct, to *this* country.

"So far as these attacks are aimed at me, *personally*, it is, I can assure you, Sir, a misconception if it be supposed I feel the venom of the darts. Within me, I have a consolation which proves an

---

1. F 33:23; 1793.
2. F 35:291; 1796.

antidote agt. their utmost malignity, rendering my mind in the retirement I have long panted after perfectly tranquil."[1]

JP: Even though you resisted inaccurate censure, were you willing to receive criticism?

GW: "It is with pleasure I receive reproof, when reproof is due, because no person can be readier to accuse me, than I am to acknowledge an error, when I am guilty of one; nor more desirous for atoning for a crime, when I am sensible of having committed it."[2]

In 1776 I asked one of my generals for strict honesty in his communication: "You cannot render a more acceptable service, nor in my estimation give a more convincing proof of your friendship, than by a free, open, and undisguised account of every matter relative to myself or [my] conduct. I can bear to hear of imputed or real errors. The man who wishes to stand well in the opinion of others must do this; because he is thereby enabled to correct his faults, or remove prejudices which are imbibed against him. For this reason, I shall thank you for giving me the opinions of the world, upon such points as you know me to be interested in; for, as I have but one capital object in view, I could wish to make my conduct coincide with the wishes of mankind, as far as I can . . . without departing from that great line of duty."[3]

And in 1778 I said to Henry Laurens, the president of the Continental Congress, "As I have no other view than to promote the public good, and am unambitious of honors not founded in the approbation of my country, I would not desire in the least degree to suppress a free spirit of enquiry into any part of my conduct that even faction itself may deem reprehensible."[4]

---

1. F 36:52; 1797.
2. F 2:122; 1757.
3. F 4:240; 1776.
4. F 10:410; 1778.

JP: So how would you answer your critics?

GW: My view was that "to persevere in one's duty and be silent is the best answer to calumny."[1]

Besides, "A mind conscious of its own rectitude fears not what is said of it, but will bid defiance to and despise shafts that are not barbed with accusations against honor or integrity."[2]

"While doing what my conscience informed me was right, as it respected my God, my country and myself, I could despise all the party clamor and unjust censure, which must be expected from some, whose personal enmity might be occasioned by their hostility to the government."[3]

JP: Did you feel, then, that being true to your conscience was paramount?

GW: In one letter I noted that "while I feel the most lively gratitude for the many instances of approbation from my country; I can no otherwise deserve it, than by obeying the dictates of my conscience."[4]

When I was still a boy I copied into my notebook: "Labor to keep alive in your breast that little spark of celestial fire, called conscience."[5]

Unfortunately, not everyone feels the same. As I observed in 1782, "Conscience . . . seldom comes to a man's aid while he is in the zenith of health and reveling in pomp and luxury upon ill-gotten spoils. It is generally the *last* act of his life, and it comes too late to be of much service to others here, or to himself hereafter."[6]

JP: How did you feel about the falsehoods that were spread about you?

---

1. F 17:225; 1779.
2. F 31:470; 1792.
3. F 30:98; 1788.
4. F 34:253; 1795.
5. Rules of Civility #110; 1745.
6. F 24:986; 1782.

GW: In general, I accepted the maxim, "Truth will ultimately prevail where pains [are] taken to bring it to light."[1]

And again: "There is but one straight course, and that is to seek truth and pursue it steadily."[2]

And, in a more philosophical mood, I said, "What can be so proper as the truth?"[3]

JP: You were much opposed to gossip.

GW: "To speak evil of any one, unless there is unequivocal proofs of their deserving it, is an injury for which there is no adequate reparation."[4]

JP: What was your view of marriage?

GW: "I have always considered marriage as the most interesting event of one's life, the foundation of happiness or misery."[5]

Indeed, "In my estimation, more permanent and genuine happiness is to be found in the sequestered walks of connubial [married] life than in the giddy rounds of promiscuous pleasure or the more tumultuous and imposing scenes of successful ambition."[6]

JP: What advice did you give in romantic matters?

GW: "Love is said to be an involuntary passion, and it is, therefore, contended that it cannot be resisted. This is true in part only, for like all things else, when nourished and supplied plentifully with aliment, it is rapid in its progress; but let these be withdrawn and it may be stifled in its birth or much stinted in its growth."[7]

---

1. F 33:465; 1794.
2. F 34:266; 1795.
3. F 2:21; 1757.
4. F 35:296; 1796.
5. F 28:152; 1785.
6. F 28:514; 1786.
7. F 35:92; 1795.

But to that I would add, "No distance can keep anxious lovers long asunder."[1]

JP: Were you one to give advice to those considering marriage?

GW: "It has ever been a maxim with me through life, neither to promote, nor to prevent a matrimonial connection, unless there should be something indispensably requiring interference in the latter. . . . To be instrumental therefore in bringing two people together who are indifferent to each other, and may soon become objects of hatred; or to prevent a union which is prompted by mutual esteem and affection, is what I never could reconcile to my feelings."[2]

"I never did, nor do I believe I ever shall, give advice to a woman who is setting out on a matrimonial voyage; first, because I never could advise one to marry without her own consent; and, secondly, I know it is to no purpose to advise her to refrain when she has obtained it. A woman very rarely asks an opinion or requires advice on such an occasion, till her resolution is formed; and then it is with the hope and expectation of obtaining a sanction, not that she means to be governed by your disapprobation, that she applies."[3]

JP: Despite that disclaimer, I believe you had some interesting observations about romantic matters.

GW: Yes. For example, I said, "A sensible woman can never be happy with a fool."[4]

And, in regard to women in society, I noted, "A woman . . . all beautiful and accomplished will, while her hand and heart are undisposed of, turn the heads and set the circle in which she

1. F 16:376; 1779.
2. F 28:152; 1783.
3. F 27:157; 1783.
4. F 34:92–93; 1795.

moves on fire. Let her marry, and what is the consequence? The madness ceases and all is quiet again. Why? Not because there is any diminution in the charms of the lady, but because there is an end of hope."[1]

Finally, I said, "It rarely happens otherwise than that a thorough-faced coquette dies in celibacy, as a punishment for her attempts to mislead others, by encouraging looks, words, or actions, given for no other purpose than to draw men on to make overtures that they may be rejected."[2]

---

1. F 34:92; 1795.
2. F 34:93; 1795.

George Washington, by Rembrandt Peale, 1795

10

A Full and Happy Life

JP: Let me ask a few questions about life and the attitudes that enrich life. What would you say is the foundation of happiness as a nation?

GW: "Nothing but harmony, honesty, industry and frugality are necessary to make us a great and happy people. Happily the present posture of affairs and the prevailing disposition of my countrymen promise to co-operate in establishing those four great and essential pillars of public felicity."[1]

"It appears to me that little more than common sense and common honesty, in the transactions of the community at large, would be necessary to make us a great and a happy nation. For if the general government, lately adopted, shall be arranged and administered in such a manner as to acquire the full confidence of the American people, I sincerely believe, they will have greater advantages, from their natural, moral and political circumstances, for public felicity, than any other people ever possessed."[2]

JP: Haven't you emphasized the relationship of morality and happiness?

GW: "The consideration that human happiness and moral duty are inseparably connected will always continue to prompt me to

---

1. F 30:186; 1789.
2. F 30:288; 1789.

promote the progress of the former by inculcating the practice of the latter."[1]

I shared this same sentiment with the people of Boston in 1789: "Your love of liberty, your respect for the laws, your habits of industry, and your practice of the moral and religious obligations are the strongest claims to national and individual happiness."[2]

JP: Most people seem to connect happiness with wealth or health or relationships.

GW: "Happiness depends more upon the internal frame of a person's own mind, than on the externals in the world."[3]

JP: Some feel their private morality doesn't matter—particularly if they are really good at what they do. For example, some of our leaders think they can cheat on their taxes. . . .

GW: "A good moral character is the first essential in a man. . . . It is therefore highly important that you should endeavor not only to be learned but virtuous."[4]

JP: Further, some leaders seem to distinguish between their private and their public behavior . . .

GW: Of course it is wrong to do so. I once wrote to a friend, "It gives me real concern to observe . . . that you should think it necessary to distinguish between my personal and public character and confine your esteem to the former."[5]

JP: What is the power of acting from principle?

GW: "In times of turbulence, when the passions are afloat, calm reason is swallowed up in the extremes to which measures are at-

1. Sparks, 12:162; 1789.
2. Sparks, 12:172; 1789.
3. F 29:162; 1787.
4. F 31:163; 1790.
5. F 3:503; 1775.

tempted to be carried; but when those subside and the empire of it is resumed, the man who acts from principle, who pursues the paths of truth, moderation and justice, will regain his influence."[1]

JP: Is it more common or rare for people to retain their virtue in the face of extreme temptation?

GW: "Few men have the virtue to withstand the highest bidder."[2]

JP: Self-control was a very important virtue to you.

GW: Yes. I said, "To be under but little or no control may be pleasing to a mind that does not reflect, but this pleasure cannot be of long duration."[3]

JP: What is the importance of controlling our thoughts?

GW: "From thinking proceeds speaking; thence to acting is often but a single step. But how irrevocable and tremendous!"[4]

JP: You have become legendary as an honest man.

GW: "I hope I shall always possess firmness and virtue enough to maintain (what I consider the most enviable of all titles) the character of *an honest man*."[5]

"My nature is open and honest and free from guile."[6]

"With my inauguration, I resolved firmly that no man should ever charge me justly with deception."[7]

"I hate deception, even where the imagination only is concerned."[8]

---

1. F 36:84; 1797.
2. F 16:119; 1779.
3. F 31:408; 1791.
4. F 28:503; 1786.
5. F 30:67; 1788.
6. F 2:18; 1757.
7. F 33:319; 1778.
8. F 16:116; 1779.

JP: Does that apply equally to governments?

GW: "It is an old adage that *honesty is the best policy*. This applies to public as well as private life, to states as well as individuals."[1]

Indeed, "Honesty will be found on every experiment, to be the best and only true policy; let us then as a nation be just."[2]

JP: How did you avoid the appearance of inappropriately being influenced?

GW: I undeviatingly followed "an established maxim . . . , not to accept a present from any one."[3]

JP: How did you feel about the fame you acquired?

GW: "The good opinion of honest men, friends to freedom and well-wishers to mankind, wherever they may be born or happen to reside, is the only kind of reputation a wise man would ever desire."[4]

JP: You had a low regard for those who gave in to vanity.

GW: I warned my nephew, "Do not conceive that fine clothes make fine men any more than fine feathers make fine birds."[5]

"I consider it an indubitable mark of mean-spiritedness and pitiful vanity to court applause from the pen or tongue of man."[6]

JP: You were a strong advocate of learning from experience.

GW: "If we cannot learn wisdom from experience, it is hard to say where it is to be found."[7]

---

1. F 28:366; 1785.
2. F 26:489; 1783.
3. F 33:433; 1794.
4. F 30:1; 1788.
5. F 26:40; 1783.
6. F 28:523; 1786.
7. F 29:312; 1787.

JP: What was your view of the passions of humankind?

GW: "The various passions and motives by which men are influenced are concomitants of fallibility, engrafted into our nature."[1]

"In the composition of the human frame there is a good deal of inflammable matter, however dormant it may lie for a time."[2]

JP: What advice would you give for a productive daily life?

GW: "Rise early, that by habit it may become familiar, agreeable, healthy, and profitable. It may, for a while, be irksome to do this, but that will wear off; and the practice will produce a rich harvest forever thereafter; whether in public or private walks of life."[3]

JP: What is your view of debt?

GW: "There is no practice more dangerous than that of borrowing money; . . . for when money can be had in this way, repayment is seldom thought of in time; the interest becomes a moth; exertions to raise it by dint of industry ceases, it comes easy and is spent freely: and many things indulged in that would never be thought of, if to be purchased by the sweat of the brow. In the meantime the debt is accumulating like a snow ball in rolling."[4]

JP: What is your opinion on gambling?

GW: A 1777 message I sent to the troops sums it up: "As few vices are attended with more pernicious consequences, in civil life; so there are none more fatal in a military one, than that of *gaming*; which often brings disgrace and ruin upon officers, and injury and punishment upon the soldiery: And reports prevailing, which, it is to be feared are too well founded, that this

---

1. F 29:357; 1788.
2. F 34:92; 1795.
3. F 36:118; 1798.
4. F 35:498; 1797.

destructive vice has spread its baneful influence in the army, and, in a peculiar manner, to the prejudice of the recruiting Service. The Commander in Chief, in the most pointed and explicit terms, forbids *all* officers and soldiers, playing at cards, dice or at any games, except those of *exercise,* for diversion; it being impossible, if the practice be allowed, at all, to discriminate between innocent play, for amusement, and criminal gaming, for pecuniary and sordid purposes. . . . The commanding officer of every corps is strictly enjoined to have this order frequently read, and strongly impressed upon the minds those under his command. Any officer, or soldier, or other person belonging to, or following, the army . . . presuming, under any pretense, to disobey this order, shall be tried by a general court martial."[1]

But this was not my view for the army alone. I also instructed my nephew, Bushrod Washington: "Avoid gaming. This is a vice which is productive of every possible evil; equally injurious to the morals and health of its votaries. It is the child of avarice, the brother of iniquity, and father of mischief. It has been the ruin of many worthy families, the loss of many a man's honor, and the cause of suicide. To all those who enter the lists, it is equally fascinating. The successful gamester pushes his good fortune, till it is overtaken by a reverse. The losing gamester, in hopes of retrieving past misfortunes, goes on from bad to worse, till grown desperate he pushes at everything and loses his all. In a word, few gain by this abominable practice, (the profit if any being diffused) while thousands are injured."[2]

JP: How strongly were you opposed to profanity?

GW: I believe the officers of the army were clear on my stand: "The General is sorry to be informed that the foolish, and wicked practice, of profane cursing and swearing (a vice heretofore little known in an American army) is growing into fashion; he hopes

1. F 8:28–29; 1777.
2. F 26:40; 1783.

the officers will, by example, as well as influence, endeavor to check it, and that both they and the men will reflect that we can have little hopes of the blessing of Heaven on our arms, if we insult it by our impiety, and folly; added to this, it is a vice so mean and low, without any temptation, that every man of sense, and character, detests and despises it."[1]

JP: What were your views on drinking alcohol?

GW: I encouraged others to "refrain from drink which is the source of all evil—and the ruin of half the workmen in this country." And I added, "An aching head and trembling limbs, which are the inevitable effects of drinking, disincline the hands from work."[2]

JP: How did you feel about following fashions?

GW: I said to my nephew, "A person who is anxious to be a leader of the fashion, or one of the first to follow it, will certainly appear in the eyes of judicious men to have nothing better than a frequent change of dress to recommend him to notice."[3]

JP: What was your approach to setting goals?

GW: "It has been a maxim with me from early life, never to undertake anything without perceiving a door to the accomplishment, in a reasonable time and with my own resources."[4]

JP: What would you say to those who are always dissatisfied with what they have—or don't have?

GW: "*Imaginary* wants are indefinite and oftentimes insatiable, because they are boundless and always changing."[5]

1. F 5:367; 1776.
2. F 30: 263–64; 1789.
3. F 30:247; 1789.
4. F 36:257–58; 1798.
5. F 26:43; 1783.

JP: Do you have any tips for those engaged in business?

GW: "If a person only sees, or directs from day to day what is to be done, business can never go on methodically or well, for in case of sickness, or the absence of the director, delays must follow. System to all things is the soul of business. To deliberate maturely, and execute promptly is the way to conduct it to advantage. With me, it has always been a maxim, rather to let my designs appear from my works than by my expressions."[1]

JP: What do you think of layers upon layers of bureaucracy?

GW: "My observation on every employment in life is that wherever and whenever one person is found adequate to the discharge of a duty by close application thereto it is worse executed by two persons, and scarcely done at all if three or more are employed therein."[2]

JP: What is your counsel about our use of time?

GW: "Time . . . is of more importance than is generally imagined."[3]

"The man who does not estimate time as money will forever miscalculate."[4]

JP: What was your formula for financial success?

GW: "A people . . . who are possessed of the spirit of commerce, who see and who will pursue their advantages may achieve almost anything."[5]

JP: What about the relationship between price and quality in purchased items?

---

1. F 36:113; 1797.
2. F 32:160; 1792.
3. F 37:460; 1799.
4. Lucas, 94; 1797.
5. F 27:473; 1784.

GW: "It is not the lowest priced goods that are always the cheapest—the quality is, or ought to be as much an object with the purchaser, as the price."[1]

JP: Many people today seem to have an entitlement mentality. When you give them help, they seem to wonder why you didn't give more or give it sooner.

GW: "Ingratitude has been experienced in all ages, and republics in particular have ever been famed for the exercise of that unnatural and sordid vice."[2]

JP: You obviously have strong feelings about ingratitude.

GW: "Nothing is a greater stranger to my breast, or a sin that my soul [more] abhors, than that black and detestable one, ingratitude."[3]

"Ingratitude . . . I hope will never constitute a part of my character, nor find a place in my bosom."[4]

JP: Do you have any advice on reading books with no real substance?

GW: "Light reading (by this, I mean books of little importance) may amuse for the moment, but leaves nothing solid behind."[5]

JP: How did you feel about reading as a means of education?

GW: "I conceive a knowledge of books is the basis upon which other knowledge is to be built."[6]

JP: You emphasized the importance of education.

GW: I advised my countrymen to "promote, . . . as an object

---

1. F 29:112; 1786.
2. F 26:462; 1783.
3. F 1:60; 1754.
4. F 11:492; 1778.
5. F 35:341; 1796.
6. F 3:50–51; 1771.

of primary importance, institutions for the general diffusion of knowledge. In proportion as the structure of a government gives force to public opinion, it is essential that public opinion should be enlightened."[1]

"Education generally [is] one of the surest means of enlightening and giving just ways of thinking to our citizens."[2]

Regarding education of the youth, I said, "The best means of forming a manly, virtuous, and happy people will be found in the right education of youth. Without this foundation, every other means, in my opinion, must fail."[3]

"A primary object . . . should be the education of our youth in the science of *government*. In a republic, what species of knowledge can be equally important? and what duty more pressing on its legislature than to patronize a plan for communicating it to those who are to be the future guardians of the liberties of the country?"[4]

"We ought to deprecate the hazard attending ardent and susceptible minds, from being too strongly, and too early prepossessed in favor of other political systems, before they are capable of appreciating their own."[5]

JP: What was your vision of the result of increased education?

GW: "I rejoice in a belief that intellectual light will spring up in the dark corners of the earth; that freedom of enquiry will produce liberality of conduct; that mankind will reverse the absurd position that the many were made for the few; and that they will not continue slaves in one part of the globe, when they can become freemen in another."[6]

---

1. F 35:230; 1796.
2. F 35:199; 1796.
3. F 28:13; 1784.
4. F 35:316; 1996.
5. F 34:106; 1795.
6. Abbot, 2:163; 1789.

JP: Do you have any advice you like to give to youth?

GW: "You are now extending into that stage of life when good or bad habits are formed. When the mind will be turned to things useful and praiseworthy, or to dissipation and vice. Fix on whichever it may, it will stick by you; for you know it has been said, and truly, "that as the twig is bent so it will grow." This, in a strong point of view, shows the propriety of letting your inexperience be directed by maturer advice, and in placing guard upon the avenues which lead to idleness and vice. The latter will approach like a thief, working upon your passions: encouraged, perhaps by bad examples: the propensity to which will increase in proportion to the practice of it and your yielding. This admonition proceeds from the purest affection for you: but I do not mean by it that you are to become a stoic, or to deprive yourself in the intervals of study of any recreations or manly exercise which reason approves."[1]

---

1. F 35:295; 1796.

George Washington, engraving from portrait by Rembrandt Peale

11

A Personal View

JP: I can tell from what you said earlier that your personal integrity was extremely important to you—and that you hoped others would know that.

GW: I underscored that toward the end of my presidency: "Conscious integrity has been my unceasing support; and while it gave me confidence in the measures I pursued, the belief of it, by acquiring to me the confidence of my fellow-citizens, ensured the success which they have had. This consciousness will accompany me in my retirement: without it, public applauses could be viewed only as proofs of public error, and felt as the upbraidings of personal demerit."[1]

And, in the last year of my life, I added, "The favorable sentiments which others, you say, have been pleased to express respecting me, cannot but be pleasing to a mind who always walked on a straight line, and endeavored as far as human frailties, and perhaps strong passions, would enable him, to discharge the relative duties to his Maker and fellowmen, without seeking any indirect or left handed attempts to acquire popularity."[2]

JP: The purity of your motives was part of that integrity.

GW: I pledged that purity in 1778: "America . . . has ever had,

1. F 35:366; 1797.
2. F 37:94–95; 1799.

and I trust she ever will have, my honest exertions to promote her interest. I cannot hope that my services have been the best; but my heart tells me they have been the best that I could render."[1]

Then, just after the Revolutionary War, I reminded General Nathanael Greene, "I bore much for the sake of peace and the public good. My conscience tells me I acted rightly in these transactions, and should they ever come to the knowledge of the world I trust I shall stand acquitted by it."[2]

In a message to Congress I gave in 1789, I said, "In executing the duties of my present important station, I can promise nothing but purity of intentions, and, in carrying these into effect, fidelity and diligence."[3]

That sentiment was reinforced in a draft of the farewell address I prepared in May 1796: "I leave you with undefiled hands—an uncorrupted heart—and with ardent vows to heaven for the welfare and happiness of that country in which I and my forefathers to the third or fourth progenitor drew our first breath."[4]

JP: You always placed integrity above popularity.

GW: "Though I prize, as I ought, the good opinion of my fellow citizens; yet, if I know myself, I would not seek or retain popularity at the expense of one social duty or moral virtue."[5]

JP: How did you balance your private desires with your public responsibilities?

GW: I said to Thomas Jefferson, "Whilst I am in office, I shall never suffer private convenience to interfere with what I conceive to be my official duties."[6]

---

1. F 11:160; 1778.
2. F 23:190; 1781.
3. F 35:411; 1789.
4. F 35:61; 1796.
5. F 30:97; 1788.
6. F 34:255; 1795.

JP: What was your policy in regard to giving charity to the poor?

GW: While I was away at war, I instructed the caretaker of my property: "Let the hospitality of the house, with respect to the poor, be kept up; let no one go hungry away. If any of these kind of people should be in want of corn, supply their necessities, provided it does not encourage them in idleness; and I have no objection to your giving my money in charity, to the amount of forty or fifty pounds a year, when you think it well bestowed. What I mean, by having no objection, is that it is my desire that it should be done. You are to consider that neither myself or wife are now in the way to do these good offices."[1]

Later, I sent this advice to my nephew: "Let your *heart* feel for the afflictions and distresses of every one, and let your *hand* give in proportion to your purse; remembering always the estimation of the widow's mite, but that it is not every one who asketh that deserveth charity; all, however, are worthy of the inquiry, or the deserving may suffer."[2]

And I advised my step-grandson (and adopted son): "Never let an indigent person ask, without receiving something, if you have the means."[3]

JP: Would you say you were more of an optimist or a pessimist?

GW: At times I felt deeply discouraged. When I was faced with the possibility of returning to arms in a possible war with France in 1798, at the age of sixty-six, I wrote, "It is in vain, I perceive, to look for ease and happiness in a world of troubles."[4]

But my more typical feeling is expressed in these words I sent to one of the generals in 1777: "We should never despair, our

---

1. F 4:115; 1775.
2. F 26:40; 1783.
3. F 35:283; 1796.
4. F 36:345; 1798.

situation before has been unpromising and has changed for the better, so I trust, it will again. If new difficulties arise, we must only put forth new exertions and proportion our efforts to the exigency of the times."[1]

That same year I said to Lafayette: "It is much to be lamented that things are not now as they formerly were; but we must not, in so great a contest, expect to meet with nothing but sun shine. I have no doubt but that everything happens so for the best; that we shall triumph over all our misfortunes, and shall, in the end, be ultimately happy; when, My Dear Marquis, if you will give me your company in Virginia, we will laugh at our past difficulties and the folly of others."[2]

Later I commended a friend "for passing the time in as merry a manner as you possibly could; it is assuredly better to go laughing than crying thro' the rough journey of life."[3]

JP: Sometimes even our best efforts don't work out. What do you tell yourself when it appears you've tried hard but still failed?

GW: "I shall not be deprived . . . of a comfort in the worst event, if I retain a consciousness of having acted to the best of my judgment."[4]

JP: As I recall, you were reluctant to accept the presidency.

GW: "Every personal consideration conspires to rivet me (if I may use the expression) to retirement. At my time of life, and under my circumstances, nothing in this world can ever draw me from it, unless it be a *conviction* that the partiality of my countrymen had made my services absolutely necessary, joined to a *fear* that my refusal might induce a belief that I preferred the

---

1. F 8:408; 1777.
2. F 10:237; 1777.
3. F 28:516; 1786.
4. F 3:297; 1775.

conservation of my own reputation and private ease, to the good of my country. After all, if I should conceive myself in a manner constrained to accept, I call Heaven to witness that this very act would be the greatest sacrifice of my personal feelings and wishes that ever I have been called upon to make."[1]

In my first inaugural address, I said, "Among the vicissitudes incident to life, no event could have filled me with greater anxieties than that of which the notification was transmitted by your order, and received on the fourteenth day of the present month. On the one hand, I was summoned by my country, whose voice I can never hear but with veneration and love, from a retreat which I had chosen with the fondest predilection, and, in my flattering hopes, with an immutable decision, as the asylum of my declining years: a retreat which was rendered every day more necessary as well as more dear to me, by the addition of habit to inclination, and of frequent interruptions in my health to the gradual waste committed on it by time. On the other hand, the magnitude and difficulty of the trust to which the voice of my country called me, being sufficient to awaken in the wisest and most experienced of her citizens, a distrustful scrutiny into his qualification, could not but overwhelm with despondence, one, who, inheriting inferior endowments from nature and unpracticed in the duties of civil administration, ought to be peculiarly conscious of his own deficiencies. In this conflict of emotions, all I dare aver is that it has been my faithful study to collect my duty from a just appreciation of every circumstance, by which it might be affected. All I dare hope is that, if in executing this task [i.e., accepting the presidency] I have been too much swayed by . . . the confidence of my fellow-citizens; and have thence too little consulted my incapacity as well as disinclination for the weighty and untried cares before me; my *error* will be palliated by the motives which

---

1. F 30:119; 1788.

misled me, and its consequences be judged by my country, with some share of the partiality in which they originated."[1]

JP: What were your feelings at the end of your presidency?

GW: "Though in reviewing the incidents of my administration, I am unconscious of intentional error, I am nevertheless too sensible of my defects not to think it probable that I may have committed many errors. Whatever they may be I fervently beseech the Almighty to avert or mitigate the evils to which they may tend. I shall also carry with me the hope that my country will never cease to view them with indulgence; and that after forty five years of my life dedicated to its service, with an upright zeal, the faults of incompetent abilities will be consigned to oblivion, as myself must soon be to the mansions of rest.

"Relying on its kindness in this as in other things, and actuated by that fervent love towards it, which is so natural to a man, who views in it the native soil of himself and his progenitors for several generations; I anticipate with pleasing expectation that retreat, in which I promise myself to realize, without alloy, the sweet enjoyment of partaking, in the midst of my fellow citizens, the benign influence of good laws under a free government, the ever favorite object of my heart, and the happy reward, as I trust, of our mutual cares, labors and dangers."[2]

JP: As president, you yearned for retirement.

GW: Shortly before the end of my second term as president I wrote, "A month from this day, if I live to see the completion of it, will place me on the wrong, perhaps it would be better to say, on the advanced, side of my grand climacteric; and although I have no cause to complain of the want of health, I can religiously aver

---

1. F 30:291; 1789.
2. F 35:237; 1796.

that no man was ever more tired of public life, or more devoutly wished for retirement, than I do."[1]

JP: Why were your memoirs not published in your lifetime?

GW: I said to my friend Dr. James Craik, "I will frankly declare to you, my dear doctor, that any memoirs of my life, distinct and unconnected with the general history of the war, would rather hurt my feelings than tickle my pride whilst I lived. I had rather glide gently down the stream of life, leaving it to posterity to think and say what they please of me, than by any act of mine to have vanity or ostentation imputed to me. I do not think vanity is a trait of my character."[2]

JP: Were you in favor of abolition of slavery?

GW: In 1786 I told my friend Robert Morris that "there is not a man living who wishes more sincerely than I do, to see a plan adopted for the abolition of it; but there is only one proper and effectual mode by which it can be accomplished, and that is by Legislative authority; and this, as far as my suffrage will go, shall never be wanting."[3]

To Lafayette, that same year: "Your late purchase of an estate in the colony of cayenne, with a view to emancipating the slaves on it, is a generous and noble proof of your humanity. Would to God a like spirit would diffuse itself generally into the minds of the people of this country; but I despair of seeing it."[4]

To John Francis Mercer, that same year: "I never mean . . . to possess another slave by purchase; it being among my first wishes to see some plan adopted by which slavery in this country may be abolished by slow, sure, and imperceptible degrees."[5]

---

1. F 34:98; 1795.
2. F 27:371; 1784.
3. F 24:408; 1786.
4. F 28:424; 1786.
5. F 29:5; 1786.

To nephew Lawrence Lewis in 1797: "I wish from my soul that the legislature of this state [Virginia] could see a policy of a gradual abolition of slavery."[1]

JP: Did you see slavery as a threat to the Union?
GW: I said in 1798, "I can clearly foresee that nothing but the rooting out of slavery can perpetuate the existence of our union, by consolidating it in a common bond of principle."[2]

JP: What were your feelings about personally owning slaves?
GW: I had one consistent message for more than two decades.
In 1778: "I every day long more and more to get clear of [my Negro slaves]."[3]
In 1794: "Were it not . . . that I am principled against selling Negros, as you would do cattle in the market, I would not, in twelve months from this date, be possessed of one, as a slave."[4]
In 1799: "On this estate (Mount Vernon) I have more working Negros by a full [half], than can be employed to any advantage. . . . [But] to sell the overplus I cannot, because I am principled against this kind of traffic in the human species. To hire them out, is almost as bad, because they could not be disposed of in families to any advantage, and to disperse the families I have an aversion."[5]
Here is what I put in my will: "Upon the decease of my wife, it is my will and desire that all the slaves which I hold in my own right shall receive their freedom. To emancipate them during her life would, though earnestly wished by me, be attended with such insuperable difficulties on account of their intermixture by marriages with the dower [inherited] Negroes as to excite the

---

1. F 36:2; 1797.
2. Bernard, 91; 1798.
3. F 12:327; 1778.
4. F 34:47; 1794.
5. F 37:338; 1799.

most painful sensations, if not disagreeable consequences from the latter, while both descriptions are in the occupancy of the same proprietor; it not being in my power, under the tenure by which the dower Negroes are held, to manumit [free] them. And whereas among those who will receive freedom according to this devise, there may be some who from old age or bodily infirmities, and others who on account of their infancy, that will be unable to support themselves; it is my will and desire that all who come under the first and second description shall be comfortably clothed and fed by my heirs while they live; and that such of the latter description as have no parents living, or if living are unable or unwilling to provide for them, shall be bound by the court until they shall arrive at the age of twenty five years; and in cases where no record can be produced whereby their ages can be ascertained, the judgment of the court upon its own view of the subject, shall be adequate and final. The Negroes thus bound are (by their masters or mistresses) to be taught to read and write and to be brought up to some useful occupation agreeably to the laws of the Commonwealth of Virginia providing for the support of orphan and other poor children. And I do hereby expressly forbid the sale or transportation out of the said commonwealth of any slave I may die possessed of, under any pretense whatsoever. And I do moreover most pointedly and most solemnly enjoin it upon my executors hereafter named, or the survivors of them, to see that this clause respecting slaves and every part thereof be religiously fulfilled at the epoch at which it is directed to take place without evasion, neglect or delay, after the crops which may then be on the ground are harvested, particularly as it respects the aged and infirm; seeing that a regular and permanent fund be established for their support so long as there are subjects requiring it, not trusting to the uncertain provision to be made by individuals. And to my mulatto man, William (calling himself William Lee), I give immediate freedom; or if he should prefer it (on account of the accidents which have rendered him incapable of walking or of any active employment) to remain in the situation he now is, it shall be optional to him to do so: In either case, however, I allow him an annuity of thirty dollars during his natural life, which shall be independent of the victuals and clothes he has been accustomed to receive, if he chooses the last alternative; but in full, with his freedom, if he prefers the first; and this I give him as a testimony of my sense of his attachment to me, and for his faithful services during the Revolutionary War."[1]

JP: I believe you considered yourself first and foremost a farmer. From your point of view in the late eighteenth century, how important was agriculture to our budding nation?

GW: While I was president I wrote, "I know of no pursuit in which more real and important services can be rendered to any country than by improving its agriculture, its breed of useful animals, and other branches of a husbandman's cares."[2]

And in one of my inaugural addresses I added, "It will not be doubted that with reference either to individual, or national welfare, agriculture is of primary importance. In proportion as nations advance in population, and other circumstances of maturity, this truth becomes more apparent; and renders the cultivation of the soil more and more, an object of public patronage."[3]

All that was consistent with something I said in an earlier letter to Lafayette, "I hope, some day or another, we shall become a storehouse and granary for the world."[4]

JP: President Washington, I am so grateful you would take this time to share your thoughts and feelings about so many things. Your wisdom will most certainly be an immense blessing

---

1. F 37:276–77; 1799.
2. F 33:437; 1794.
3. F 35:315; 1796.
4. F 29:526; 1788.

to all who read these words. Do you have any parting counsel for your fellow Americans in the twenty-first century?

GW: I think I would repeat the words of the first Thanksgiving Proclamation I issued as president, a little of which I have already quoted: "Whereas it is the duty of all nations to acknowledge the providence of Almighty God, to obey his will, to be grateful for his benefits, and humbly to implore his protection and favor, and Whereas both houses of Congress have by their joint committee requested me 'to recommend to the people of the United States a day of public thanksgiving and prayer to be observed by acknowledging with grateful hearts the many signal favors of Almighty God, especially by affording them an opportunity peaceably to establish a form of government for their safety and happiness.'

"Now therefore I do recommend and assign Thursday the 26th day of November next to be devoted by the people of these states to the service of that great and glorious Being, who is the beneficent Author of all the good that was, that is, or that will be. That we may then all unite in rendering unto him our sincere and humble thanks, for his kind care and protection of the people of this country previous to their becoming a nation, for the signal and manifold mercies, and the favorable interpositions of his providence, which we experienced in the course and conclusion of the late war, for the great degree of tranquility, union, and plenty, which we have since enjoyed, for the peaceable and rational manner in which we have been enabled to establish constitutions of government for our safety and happiness, and particularly the national one now lately instituted, for the civil and religious liberty with which we are blessed, and the means we have of acquiring and diffusing useful knowledge and in general for all the great and various favors which he hath been pleased to confer upon us.

"And also that we may then unite in most humbly offering our prayers and supplications to the great Lord and Ruler of Nations and beseech him to pardon our national and other transgressions, to enable us all, whether in public or private stations, to perform our several and relative duties properly and punctually, to render our national government a blessing to all the people, by constantly being a government of wise, just and constitutional laws, discreetly and faithfully executed and obeyed, to protect and guide all sovereigns and nations (especially such as have shown kindness unto us) and to bless them with good government, peace, and concord. To promote the knowledge and practice of true religion and virtue, and the increase of science among them and us, and generally to grant unto all mankind such a degree of temporal prosperity as he alone knows to be best."[1]

---

1. F 30:427; 1789.

George Washington, by Gilbert Stuart, about 1821

Epilogue

For two centuries after America's founding, George Washington was a hero of many schoolchildren (and some adults). They thrilled at stories of his bravery. They loved to hear about how he led the "ragtag" American armies, against all odds, to defeat the strongest nation on earth.

But in the twentieth century, a new school of historians set themselves to "correct" history. Often cynical, some of these revisionist historians decided to "set the record straight" about America's Founding Fathers. Many of the new interpretations seemed to take pains to humanize these men more—to point out their flaws.

In my reading of the lives of the Founders, it is clear that they were indeed less than perfect. It is also clear that most of them were truly extraordinary men. They would stand as titans in any age.

Such a man was George Washington. He was larger than life. He stood physically taller than most of his contemporaries. He also was of heroic size in his character, his integrity, his determination to follow the right course in life, his willingness to sacrifice for the cause of freedom. He was a leader who inspired unusual confidence in those who followed him. He was a man who cherished his good standing before God.

Meeting George Washington through his writings and the stories of his life has been one of the great experiences of my life. I regard him as one of the greatest of all Americans. I consider him to be one of the greatest men who ever lived.

In these days, the United States of America is going through difficult times. The federal government has grown in size, power, and reach far beyond what the Founders envisioned. In some people, greed has replaced wisdom in financial dealings. Some citizens have turned their backs on proven moral values, feeling them old fashioned.

George Washington's example stands as a beacon to our times—with his public and private morality, wise political philosophy, temperance, and adherence to the principles of a democratic republic shining before us. As do his words, spoken not on the basis of theory but practical experience in the challenging school of life. In these troubled times, following the Father of Our Country may be the smartest thing we could ever do.

George Washington at Princeton,
by Charles Willson Peale, 1779

George Washington as Seen by Those Who Knew Him

After having had the singular experience of spending many hours in interview with President Washington, I was surprised to be visited by a number of men and women who knew him. Some were close friends; some had spent only an afternoon with him. All were eager to tell me their impressions of one of the greatest men of their age. I have arranged them in order of the date of their reminiscence and have included a brief background note on each the first time he or she is quoted. I have also standardized spelling and capitalization.

OFFICERS OF THE VIRGINIA REGIMENT, 1758

"We your most obedient and affectionate officers, beg leave to express our great concern, at the disagreeable news we have received of your determination to resign the command of that corps, in which we have under you long served.

"The happiness we have enjoyed, and the honor we have acquired, together with the mutual regard that has always subsisted between you and your officers, have implanted so sensible an affection in the minds of us all, that we cannot be silent on this critical occasion.

"In our earliest infancy you took us under your tuition, trained us up in the practice of that discipline, which alone can constitute good troops, from the punctual observance of which you never suffered the least deviation.

"Your steady adherence to impartial justice, your quick discernment and invariable regard to merit, wisely intended to inculcate those genuine sentiments, of true honor and passion for glory, from which the great military achievements have been derived, first heightened our natural emulation, and our desire to excel. . . .

"Judge then, how sensibly we must be affected with the loss of such an excellent commander, such a sincere friend, and so affable a companion. How rare is it to find those amiable qualifications blended together in one man! How great the loss of such a man! . . .

"Frankness, sincerity, and a certain openness of soul, are the true characteristics of an officer, and we flatter ourselves that you do not think us capable of saying anything, contrary to the purest dictates of our minds. Fully persuaded of this, we beg leave to assure you, that as you have hitherto been the actuating soul of the whole corps, we shall at all times pay the most invariable regard to your will and pleasure, and will always be happy to demonstrate by our actions, with how much respect and esteem we are,

"Sir. Your most affectionate and most obedient humble servants"[1]

CHARLES WILLSON PEALE, 1773

"One afternoon several young gentlemen, visitors at Mount Vernon, and myself were engaged in pitching the bar, one of the athletic sports common in those days, when suddenly the colonel [Washington] appeared among us. He requested to be shown the

---

1. *Records of the Columbia Historical Society*, 1:24–26. This quotation is from a letter of appreciation Washington's officers wrote to him when he resigned his commission as commander of the Virginia regiment in December 1758.

pegs that marked the bounds of our efforts; then, smiling, and without putting off his coat, held out his hand for the missile. No sooner did the heavy iron bar feel the grasp of his mighty hand than it lost the power of gravitation and whizzed through the air, striking the ground far, very far, beyond our utmost limits. We were indeed amazed as we stood around, all stripped to the buff, with shirt-sleeves rolled up, and having thought ourselves very clever fellows; while the Colonel, on retiring, pleasantly observed, 'When you beat my pitch, young gentlemen, I'll try again.'"[1]

Eliphalet Dyer, 1775

"He seems discrete and virtuous, no harum-scarum, ranting swearing fellow, but sober, steady, and calm. His modesty will induce him I dare say to take and order every step with the best advice possible to be obtained in the army."[2]

John Adams, 1775

"He is brave, wise, generous and humane."[3]

---

1. Custis, 519. Charles Willson Peale, 1741–1827, was a painter who produced nearly sixty portraits of George Washington, three of which are found in this volume.

2. Burnett, 1:128. Eliphalet Dyer, 1721–1807, served in the Continental Congress at the same time as Washington.

3. Ryerson, 33. John Adams, 1735–1826, served in the Continental Congress with George Washington, was a signer of the Declaration of Independence, and later served as vice president during both of Washington's terms as president; he served as the second president of the United States.

THOMAS CUSHING JR., 1775

"He is a complete gentleman. He is sensible, amiable, virtuous, modest, and brave."[1]

CHARLES CARROLL OF ANNAPOLIS, 1775

"We know him to be a cool, prudent man."[2]

ABIGAIL ADAMS, 1775

"I was struck with General Washington. You had prepared me to entertain a favorable opinion of him, but I thought the one half was not told me. Dignity with ease, and complacency, the gentleman and soldier look agreeably blended in him. Modesty marks every line and feature of his face."[3]

BENJAMIN RUSH, 1775

"General Washington . . . seems to be one of those illustrious heroes whom providence raises up once in three or four hundred years to save a nation from ruin. If you do not know his person, perhaps you will be pleased to hear that he has so much martial dignity in his deportment that you would distinguish him to be a general and a soldier from among ten thousand people. There is

1. Hatch, 12. Thomas Cushing Jr., 1725–1788, served in the Continental Congress at the same time as Washington.

2. Smith, 132. Charles Carroll of Annapolis, 1702–1782, was the father of Charles Carroll of Carrollton, 1737–1832, one of the signers of the Declaration of Independence.

3. Adams, 1:51–52. Abigail Adams, 1744–1818, was the wife of John Adams, who served as vice president under President George Washington. She later became the second First Lady of the United States. This description was included in a letter to her husband, John Adams.

not a king in Europe that would not look like a valet de chamber by his side."[1]

SAMUEL SHAW, 1777

"Our army love our General very much, but yet they have one thing against him, which is the little care he takes of himself in any action. His personal bravery, and the desire he has of animating his troops by example, make him fearless of any danger. This, while it makes him appear great, occasions us much uneasiness. But Heaven, who has hitherto been his shield, I hope will still continue to guard so valuable a life."[2]

WILLIAM HOOPER, 1777

"Will posterity believe the tale? When it shall be consistent with policy to give the history of that man from his first introduction into our service, how often America has been rescued from ruin by the mere strength of his genius, conduct, and courage, encountering every obstacle that want of money, men, arms, ammunition, could throw in his way, an impartial world will say with you that he is the greatest man on earth. Misfortunes are the element in which he shines; they are the groundwork on which his picture appears to the greatest advantage. He rises superior to them all; they serve as foils to his fortitude and as stimulants to bring into view those great qualities which his modesty keeps

---

1. Butterfield, 1:92. Benjamin Rush, 1746–1813, a signer of the Declaration of Independence, served as surgeon general for the continental army.
2. Quincy, 29–30. Samuel Shaw, 1754–1794, served as a major and aide-de-camp to General Henry Knox during the Revolutionary War.

concealed. I could fill the side in his praise; but anything I can say cannot equal his merits."[1]

ROBERT MORRIS, 1777

"Heaven, no doubt for the noblest purposes, has blessed you with a firmness of mind, steadiness of countenance, and patience in sufferings, that give you infinite advantages over other men."[2]

JOHN ADAMS, 1777

"I thought him a perfectly honest man, with an amiable and excellent heart, and the most important character at that time among us, for he was the center of our union."[3]

MARQUIS DE LAFAYETTE, 1777

"Our general is a man truly made for this revolution, which could not succeed without him. . . . I admire him more each day for the beauty of his character and his spirit. . . . His name will be revered down through the centuries by all those who love liberty and humanity."[4]

---

1. Bancroft, 5:110. William Hooper, 1742–1790, a signer of the Declaration of Independence, served with Washington in the Continental Congress.

2. Sparks, 4:339. Robert Morris, 1734–1806, was a signer of the Declaration of Independence and the U.S. Constitution. Washington stayed at his home during the Constitutional Convention. This comment was included in a letter Morris sent to George Washington.

3. Adams, 3:92.

4. Tower, 1:243. Marquis de Lafayette, 1757–1834, was a general in the American Revolutionary War; he became one of Washington's closest associates.

JONATHAN WILLIAMS AUSTIN, 1778

"Our exalted general . . . seems to have been raised up by heaven, to show to what an height humanity may soar; who generously sacrificing affluence and domestic ease, wishes to share with you in every danger and distress."[1]

MARQUIS DE LAFAYETTE, 1778

"Every noble and sensitive soul must love the excellent qualities of his heart. . . . His honesty, his candor, his sensitivity, his virtue in the full sense of the word are above all praise."[2]

JAMES THACHER, 1778

"The personal appearance of our commander in chief, is that of the perfect gentleman and accomplished warrior. He is remarkably tall, full six feet, erect and well proportioned. The strength and proportion of his joints and muscles, appear to be commensurate with the preeminent powers of his mind. The serenity of his countenance, and majestic gracefulness of his deportment, impart a strong impression of that dignity and grandeur, which are his peculiar characteristics, and no one can stand in his presence without feeling the ascendancy of his mind, and associating with his countenance the idea of wisdom, philanthropy, magnanimity, and patriotism. There is a fine symmetry in the features of his face, indicative of a benign and dignified spirit. His nose is straight, and his eyes inclined to blue. He wears his hair in a becoming cue, and from his forehead it is turned back and powdered in a manner which adds to the military air of his appear-

---

1. Niles, 36. Jonathan Williams Austin, 1751–1779, served as a law clerk to John Adams and later as a lawyer himself.
2. Kaminski, 478.

ance. He displays a native gravity, but devoid of all appearance of ostentation. His uniform dress is a blue coat, with two brilliant epaulettes, buff colored under clothes, and a three cornered hat, with a black cockade. He is constantly equipped with an elegant small sword, boots, and spurs, in readiness to mount his noble charger. There is not in the present age, perhaps, another man so eminently qualified to discharge the arduous duties of the exalted station he is called to sustain, amidst difficulties which to others would appear insurmountable, nor could any man have more at command the veneration and regard of the officers and soldiers of our army, even after defeat and misfortune. This is the illustrious chief, whom a kind Providence has decreed as the instrument to conduct our country to peace and to independence.

"His Excellency, made a visit to our hospital; his arrival was scarcely announced, before he presented himself at our doors. Dr. Williams and myself had the honor to wait on this great and truly good man, through the different wards, and to reply to his inquiries relative to the condition of our patients. He appeared to take a deep interest in the situation of the sick and wounded soldiers, and inquired particularly as to their treatment and comfortable accommodations."[1]

MOSES HAZEN, 1780

"[General Washington] is the very idol of his country, and who I love, regard, and esteem, as one of the best men since the creation of Adam."[2]

---

1. Baker, 9–10. James Thacher, 1754–1844, served as a surgeon during the Revolutionary War.
2. Kaminski, 481. Moses Hazen, 1733–1803, was a brigadier general who served with Washington during the Revolutionary War.

NATHANAEL GREENE, 1781

"General Washington's influence will do more than all the assemblies upon the continent. I always thought him exceedingly popular; but in many places he is little less than adored, and universally admired. From being the friend of the general I found myself exceedingly well received; but more from being the friend of the General's than from my own merit."[1]

MATHIEU, COUNT DUMAS, 1781

"General Washington, accompanied by the Marquis de la Fayette, repaired in person to the French headquarters. We had been impatient to see the hero of liberty. His dignified address, his simplicity of manners, and mild gravity, surpassed our expectation, and won every heart. After having conferred with Count Rochambeau, as he was leaving us to return to his headquarters near West Point, I received the welcome order to accompany him as far as Providence. We arrived there at night; the whole of the population had assembled from the suburbs, we were surrounded by a crowd of children carrying torches, reiterating the acclamations of the citizens; all were eager to approach the person of him whom they called their father, and pressed so closely around us that they hindered us from proceeding. General Washington was much affected, stopped a few moments, and pressing my hand, said, 'We may be beaten by the English; it is the chance of war; but behold an army which they can never conquer.' . . .

"I here interrupt the succinct narrative of the most remarkable events of the winter of 1781, to recall the impressions which I received during the short stay that I made in the family of the deliverer of America. The brilliant actions of great men cannot

---

1. Hamilton, 1:204. Nathanael Greene, 1742–1786, was a major general who served with Washington during the Revolutionary War.

fail to be recalled by history; the anecdotes of their private life are equally worthy of being preserved because they often make us better acquainted with the principal traits of their character. The general gave me a most cordial reception. . . . Being invited to dinner, which was remarkably plain, I had leisure to admire the perfect harmony of his noble and fine countenance, with the simplicity of his language and the justice and depth of his observations. He generally sat long at table, and animated the conversation by unaffected cheerfulness."[1]

Marquis de Lafayette, 1781

"As for the commander in chief, his genius, his greatness, and the nobility of his manners attach to him the hearts and veneration of both [American and French] armies."[2]

John Jay, 1781

"If Providence shall be pleased to lead him, with safety and success, through all the duties of his station, and carry him home with the blessings of America on his head, I think he will exhibit to the world the most singular instance of virtue, greatness, and good-fortune united which the history of mankind has hitherto recorded."[3]

---

1. Baker, 211–15. Mathieu, Count Dumas, 1753–1837, a native of France, served as aide-de-camp to Rochambeau during the American Revolutionary War.

2. Clary, 341.

3. Johnston, 2:159. John Jay, 1745–1829, served in the Continental Congress at the same time as George Washington. President Washington later named him the first Chief Justice of the United States.

Stephen Higginson, 1783

"Three days we spent at headquarters with General Washington, with whose steadiness and great prudence I was much pleased; he surely was made expressly for these times, and no other character could have answered our purpose."[1]

John Adams, 1783

"His character . . . is above all praise, as every character whose rule and object are duty, not interest nor glory, which I think has been strictly true with the general from the beginning, and I trust will continue to the end."[2]

Marquis de Lafayette, 1783

"In every instance, my dear General, I have the satisfaction to love and to admire you. The conduct you had on that occasion [the victory over] was highly praised throughout all Europe, and your returning to a private station is called the finishing stroke to an unparalleled character. Never did a man exist who so honorably stood in the opinions of mankind, and your name, if possible, will become still greater in posterity. Everything that is great, and everything that is good were not hitherto united in one man. Never did one man live whom the soldier, statesman, patriot, and philosopher could equally admire, and never was a revolution brought about, that in its motives, its conduct, and its consequences could so well immortalize its glorious chief. I am proud of you, my dear General, your glory makes me feel as if it

1. Kaminski, 483. Stephen Higginson, 1743–1828, was a Boston merchant and shipmaster; he served in the Confederation Congress at the time of this visit with Washington.
2. Adams, 8:73.

was my own—and while the world is gaping at you, I am pleased to think, and to tell, the qualities of your heart do render you still more valuable than anything you have done."[1]

ELKANAH WATSON, 1785

"To have communed with such a man in the bosom of his family I shall always regard as one of the highest privileges and most cherished incidents of my life. I found him kind and benignant in the domestic circle, revered and beloved by all around him, agreeably social, without ostentation; delighting in anecdote and adventures, without assumption; his domestic arrangements harmonious and systematic. . . .

"The first evening I spent under the wing of his hospitality we sat a full hour at table, by ourselves, without the least interruption, after the family had retired. I was extremely oppressed with a severe cold and excessive coughing, contracted from the exposure of a harsh winter journey. He pressed me to use some remedies, but I declined doing so. As usual after retiring my cough increased. When some time had elapsed the door of my room was gently opened, and on drawing my bed-curtains, to my utter astonishment, I beheld Washington himself standing at my bedside with a bowl of hot tea in his hand. I was mortified and distressed beyond expression. This little incident, occurring in common life with an ordinary man would not have been noticed, but as a trait of the benevolence and the private virtue of Washington it deserves to be recorded."[2]

---

1. Kaminski, 486.
2. Schroeder, 2:1530–31. Elkanah Watson, 1758–1842, born in Plymouth, Massachusetts, was a traveler and a writer who met with Washington in January 1785.

ROBERT HUNTER JR., 1785

"The general is about six foot high, perfectly straight and well made, rather inclined to be lusty. His eyes are full and blue and seem to express an air of gravity. His nose inclines to the aquiline; his mouth small; his teeth are yet good; and his cheeks indicate perfect health. His forehead is a noble one, and he wears his hair turned back, without curls (quite in the officer's style) and tied in a long queue behind. Altogether, he makes a most noble, respectable appearance, and I really think him the first man in the world. . . .

"He is one of the most regular men in the world. When no particular company is at his house, he goes to bed always at nine and gets up with the sun. It's astonishing the packets of letters that daily come for him, from all parts of the world, which employ him most of the morning to answer, and his secretary Mr. [William] Shaw to copy and arrange. The General has all the accounts of the war yet to settle. Shaw tells me he keeps as regular books as any merchant whatever, and a daily journal of all his transactions. It's amazing the number of letters he wrote during the war. . . .

"He never undertakes anything without having first well considered of it and consulted different people. But when once he has begun anything, no obstacle or difficulty can come in his way but what he is determined to surmount. . . .

"The colonel and I had our horses ready after dinner to return to Alexandria, and notwithstanding all we could do, the general absolutely insisted upon our staying, on account of the bad afternoon. We therefore complied . . . as I could not refuse the pressing and kind invitation of so great a general. Though our greatest enemy, I admire him as superior even to the Roman heroes themselves."[1]

---

1. Hunter, 17:76–78. Robert Hunter Jr., 1764–1843, was a young merchant from London who traveled in Canada and the United States in 1785–1786.

MARQUIS DE CHASTELLUX, 1786

"Here would be the proper place to give the portrait of General Washington. . . . The strongest characteristic of this respectable man is the perfect union which reigns between the physical and moral qualities which compose the individual, one alone will enable you to judge of all the rest. . . . Brave without temerity, laborious without ambition, generous without prodigality, noble without pride, virtuous without severity. . . . This is the seventh year that he has commanded the army, and that he has obeyed the Congress; more need not be said, especially in America, where they know how to appreciate all the merit contained in this simple fact. . . . It will be said of him, AT THE END OF A LONG CIVIL WAR, HE HAD NOTHING WITH WHICH HE COULD REPROACH HIMSELF. If anything can be more marvelous than such a character, it is the unanimity of the public suffrages in his favor. Soldier, magistrate, people, all love and admire him; all speak of him in terms of tenderness and veneration. . . .

"In speaking of this perfect whole of which General Washington furnishes the idea, I have not excluded exterior form. His stature is noble and lofty, he is well made, and exactly proportioned; his physiognomy mild and agreeable, but such as to render it impossible to speak particularly of any of his features, so that in quitting him, you have only the recollection of a fine face. He has neither a grave nor a familiar face, his brow is sometimes marked with thought, but never with inquietude; in inspiring respect, he inspires confidence, and his smile is always the smile of benevolence."[1]

---

1. Baker, 26–28. Francois Jean, Marquis de Chastellux, 1734–1788, served as a major general under the Count de Rochambeau during the Revolutionary War; Chastellux served as the principal liaison officer between Rochambeau and Washington.

GOUVERNEUR MORRIS, 1787

"I have observed that your name to the new Constitution has been of infinite service. Indeed, I am convinced that, if you had not attended that Convention, and the same paper had been handed out to the world, it would have met with a colder reception, with fewer and weaker advocates, and with more, and more strenuous, opponents. As it is, should the idea prevail that you will not accept the presidency, it would prove fatal in many parts. The truth is, that your great and decided superiority leads men willingly to put you in a place which will not add to your personal dignity, nor raise you higher than you already stand. But they would not readily put any other person in the same situation. . . .

I will add my conviction that of all men you are best fitted to fill that office. Your steady temper is *indispensably necessary* to give a firm and manly tone to the new government. To constitute a well-poised political machine is the task of no common workman; but to set it in motion requires still greater qualities. . . . No constitution is the same on paper and in life. The exercise of authority depends on personal character; and the whip and reins by which an able charioteer governs unruly steeds will only hurl the unskillful presumer with more speedy and headlong violence to the earth. The horses once trained may be managed by a woman or a child; not so when they first feel the bit. And indeed among these thirteen horses now about to be coupled together there are some of every race and character. They will listen to your voice, and submit to your control; you therefore must I say must mount the seat. That the result may be as pleasing to you as it will be useful to them I wish but do not expect. You will however on this, as on other occasions, feel that interior satisfaction and self-approbation which the world cannot give; and you will have in every possible event the applause of those who know you enough to respect you properly."[1]

BRISSOT DE WARVILLE, 1788

"You have heard me criticize M. Chastellux for having put so much art in his character sketch of the general. To paint a pretentious portrait of an unpretentious man is nonsense. The general's kindness of heart shines in his eyes, which, although they no longer have the piercing gleam his officers knew when he was at the head of the army, still grow animated in conversation. His face has no distinctive features, which is why it has always been difficult to paint a good likeness of him, and why few of his portraits resemble him. His answers to queries are full of common sense. He is very cautious and hesitant about committing himself, but once he has made a decision he is firm and unshakable. His modesty is astonishing, particularly to a Frenchman. He speaks of the American war as if he had not been its leader, and of his victories with a greater indifference than even a foreigner would. I saw him lose his characteristic composure and become heated only when he talked about the present state of affairs in America. The schisms within his country torture his soul, and he feels the necessity of rallying all lovers of liberty around one central issue, the need to strengthen the government. He is still ready to sacrifice his peaceful life, which gives him such happiness. 'Happiness like this,' he told me, 'is not to be found in great honors or in the tumult of life.' This philosopher believed in this truth so strongly that from the moment of his retirement he severed every political connection and renounced all offices. And yet, despite his spirit of abnegation, his disinterestedness, and his modesty, this

---

1. *Documentary History*, 4:359–60. Gouverneur Morris, 1752–1816, was a lawyer from New York who served in the Continental Congress and later the Constitutional Convention; he put much of the new Constitution in its final form. These comments were included in a letter to George Washington.

astonishing man has enemies! He has been viciously attacked in the newspapers and has been accused of being ambitious and conniving, when all his life, when indeed all America, can testify to his selflessness and integrity. Virginia is perhaps the only state where he does have enemies, for everywhere else I have heard his name pronounced with nothing but respect mingled with affection and gratitude. Americans speak of him as they would of a father. Perhaps Washington is not to be compared to the most famous military leaders, but he has all the qualities and all the virtues of the perfect republican."[1]

JEDIDIAH MORSE, 1789

"No person who had not the advantage of being present when General Washington received the intelligence of peace, and who did not accompany him to his domestic retirement, can describe the relief which that joyful event brought to his laboring mind, or the supreme satisfaction with which he withdrew to private life. . . . Here a minuter description of his domestic life may be expected.

"To apply a life, at best but short, to the most useful purposes, he lives as he ever has done, in the unvarying habits of regularity, temperance, and industry. He rises, in winter as well as summer, at the dawn of day; and generally reads or writes some time before breakfast. He breakfasts about seven o'clock on three small Indian hoe-cakes, and as many dishes of tea. He rides immediately to his different farms, and remains with his laborers until a little past two o clock, when he returns and dresses. At three he dines, commonly on a single dish, and drinks from half a pint to a pint of Madeira wine. This, with one small glass of

---

1. Kaminski, 498–99. Brissot de Warville, 1754–1793, was a French writer who described his meeting with Washington in a book he published called *New Travels in the United States of America*.

punch, a draught of beer, and two dishes of tea (which he takes half an hour before sun-setting) constitutes his whole sustenance till the next day. Whether there be company or not, the table is always prepared, by its elegance and exuberance, for their reception; and the general remains at it for an hour after dinner, in familiar conversation and convivial hilarity. It is then that everyone present is called upon to give some absent friend as a toast; the name not infrequently awakens a pleasing remembrance of past events, and gives a new turn to the animated colloquy. General Washington is more cheerful than he was in the army. Although his temper is rather of a serious cast, and his countenance commonly carries the impression of thoughtfulness, yet he perfectly relishes a pleasant story, an unaffected sally of wit, or a burlesque description, which surprises by its suddenness and incongruity with the ordinary appearance of the object described. After this sociable and innocent relaxation, he applies himself to business, and about nine o'clock retires to rest. This is the routine, and this the hour he observes, when no one but his family is present; at other times, he attends politely upon his company until they wish to withdraw.

"Notwithstanding he has no offspring, his actual family consists of eight persons. (The family of General Washington, in addition to the general and his lady, consists of Major George Washington [nephew to the general and late aide de camp to the Marquis de la Fayette], with his wife, who is a niece to the general's lady, Col. Humphreys, formerly aide de camp to the general, Mr. Lear, a gentleman of literal education, private secretary to the general, and two grandchildren of Mrs. Washington.) It is seldom alone. He keeps a pack of hounds, and in the season indulges himself with hunting once in a week; at which diversion the gentlemen of Alexandria often assist.

"Agriculture is the favorite employment of General Washington, in which he wishes to pass the remainder of his days. To acquire and communicate practical knowledge, he corresponds with . . . many agricultural gentlemen in this country. As improvement is known to be his passion, he receives envoys with rare seeds and results of new projects from every quarter. He likewise makes copious notes, relative to his own experiments, the state of the seasons, the nature of soils, the effects of different kinds of manure, and such other topics as may throw light on the farming business.

"On Saturday in the afternoon, every week, reports are made by all his overseers, and registered in books kept for the purpose: so that at the end of the year, the quantity of labor and produce may be accurately known. Order and economy are established in all the departments within and without doors. His lands are enclosed in lots of equal dimensions, and crops are assigned to each for many years. Everything is undertaken on a great scale; but with a view to introduce or augment the culture of such articles as he conceives will become most beneficial in their consequence to the country. He has raised this year, two hundred lambs, sowed twenty-seven bushels of flax seed, and planted more than seven hundred bushels of potatoes. In the meantime, the public may rest persuaded, that there is manufactured under his roof, linen and woolen cloth, nearly or quite sufficient for the use of his numerous household."[1]

FISHER AMES, 1789

"I was present in the pew with the president [at Washington's inauguration], and must assure you that, after making all deductions for the delusion of one's fancy in regard to characters, I still think of him with more veneration than for any other person. Time has made havoc upon his face. That, and many other

1. Baker, 30–34. Jedidiah Morse, 1761–1826, an educator and minister from Connecticut, was also the author of a number of geography textbooks; he has been called the father of American geography. This biographical sketch was included in one of Morse's geography books.

circumstances not to be reasoned about, conspire to keep up the awe which I brought with me. He addressed the two Houses in the Senate-chamber; it was a very touching scene, and quite of a solemn kind. His aspect grave, almost to sadness; his modesty, actually shaking; his voice deep, a little tremulous, and so low as to call for close attention; added to the series of objects presented to the mind, and overwhelming it, produced emotions of the most affecting kind upon the members. I . . . sat entranced. It seemed to me an allegory in which Virtue was personified, and addressing those whom she would make her votaries. Her power over the heart was never greater, and the illustration of her doctrine by her own example was never more perfect."[1]

Samuel Nasson, 1789

"They praise your president to me for all his virtues. . . . They almost adore him and I join with them and could almost fill a volume with his virtues but why should I attempt to paint the sun?"[2]

Abigail Adams, 1789

"Our august president is a singular example of modesty and diffidence. He has a dignity which forbids familiarity mixed with an easy affability which creates love and reverence."[3]

---

1. Ames, 1:34. Fisher Ames, 1758–1808, was a great orator and lawyer from Massachusetts; he served in Congress during the same years Washington served as president.

2. Jensen, 582–83. Samuel Nasson, 1744–1800, served as a major in the Revolutionary War; afterwards, he served as a local politician and businessman in Maine and Massachusetts.

3. Whitney, 233.

Abigail Adams, 1790

"[Washington] has so happy a faculty of appearing to accommodate and yet carrying his point, that if he was not really one of the best intentioned men in the world he might be a very dangerous one. He is polite with dignity, affable without familiarity, distant without haughtiness, grave without austerity, modest, wise and good. These are traits in his character which peculiarly fit him for the exalted station he holds, and God grant that he may hold it with the same applause and universal satisfaction for many many years, as it is my firm opinion that no other man could rule over this great people and consolidate them into one mighty empire but he who is set over us."[1]

Francois Auguste, Vicomte de Chateaubriand, 1791

"Something of stillness envelopes the actions of Washington; he acts deliberately: you would say that he feels himself to be the representative of the liberty of future ages, and that he is afraid of compromising it. It is not his own destinies but those of his country with which this hero of a new kind is charged; he allows not himself to hazard what does not belong to him. But what light bursts forth from this profound obscurity! Search the unknown forests where glistened the sword of Washington, what will you find there? graves? no! a world! Washington has left the United States for a trophy of his field of battle.

"Bonaparte has not any one characteristic of this grave American . . . ; he wishes to create nothing but his own renown; he takes upon himself nothing but his own aggrandizement. . . .

"Each is rewarded according to his works: Washington raises his nation to independence: a retired magistrate he sinks quietly

---

1. McCullough, 413.

to rest beneath his paternal roof, amid the regrets of his countrymen and the veneration of all nations. . . .

"Washington and Bonaparte sprang from the bosom of a republic: both born of liberty, the one was faithful to it, the other
betrayed it. Their lot in futurity will be as different as their choice.

"The name of Washington will spread with liberty from age to
age; it will mark the commencement of a new era for mankind.
. . .

"Washington was completely the representative of the wants,
the ideas, the knowledge, and the opinions of his time; he sec-
onded instead of thwarting the movement of mind; he aimed at
that which it was his duty to aim at: hence the coherence and the
perpetuity of his work. This man, who appears not very striking,
because he is natural and in his just proportions, blended his
existence with that of his country; his glory is the common patri-
mony of growing civilization: his renown towers like one of those
sanctuaries, whence flows an inexhaustible spring for the people.

"Such was my interview with the man who gave liberty to a
whole world. Washington sunk into the tomb before any little
celebrity had attached to my name. I passed before him as the
most unknown of beings; he was in all his glory, I in the depth
of my obscurity. My name probably dwelt not a whole day in
his memory. Happy, however, that his looks were cast upon me!
I have felt myself warmed for it all the rest of my life. There is a
virtue in the looks of a great man."[1]

JAMES KENT, 1793

"I visited the president at one of his public levees. . . . The
president was dressed in a suit of plain cloth of a snuff color,

---

1. Baker, 182–85. Francois Auguste, Vicomte de Chateaubriand, 1768–1848,
was a celebrated French author who visited the United States—and President
Washington—in 1791.

with silk stockings, and a sword by his side. His manners were easy, but distant and reserved. His eye was expressive of mildness and reflection. His person was tall and full of dignity. No person can approach him without being penetrated with respect and reverence. Without the brilliancy of Caesar's talents, or the daring exertions of Frederick, such has been his steadiness, discretion, good sense, and integrity that no man ever attained a greater ascendency over free minds or ever reigned so long and so completely in the hearts of a sober and intelligent people."[1]

HENRY WANSEY, 1794

"[On] June 6, I had the honor of an interview with the President of the United States, to whom I was introduced by Mr. Dandridge, his secretary. He received me very politely, and after reading my letters, I was asked to breakfast. There was very little of the ceremony of courts, the Americans will not permit this; nor does the disposition of his Excellency lead him to assume it.

"I confess, I was struck with awe and veneration, when I recollected that I was now in the presence of one of the greatest men upon earth the GREAT WASHINGTON the noble and wise benefactor of the world! . . . When we look down from this truly great and illustrious character, upon other public servants, we find a glaring contrast; nor can we fix our attention upon any other great men, without discovering in them a vast and mortifying dissimilarity!

"The president in his person, is tall and thin, but erect; rather of an engaging than a dignified presence. He appears very thoughtful, is slow in delivering himself, which occasions some to conclude him reserved, but it is rather, I apprehend, the effect of much thinking and reflection, for there is great appearance to me of affability and accommodation. He was at this time in his

---

1. Kent, 61. James Kent, 1763–1847, was an American jurist, legal scholar, and local politician from New York.

sixty-third year, being born February 11, 1732, O. S. but he has very little the appearance of age, having been all his life-time so exceeding temperate. There is a certain anxiety visible in his countenance, with marks of extreme sensibility."[1]

THOMAS JEFFERSON, 1795

"[The president] errs as other men do, but errs with integrity."[2]

ISAAC WELD, 1796

"On this day (February 22, 1796) General Washington terminated his sixty-fourth year; but though not an unhealthy man, he seemed considerably older. The innumerable vexations he has met with in his different public capacities have very sensibly impaired the vigor of his constitution, and given him an aged appearance. There is a very material difference, however, in his looks when seen in private and when he appears in public full dress; in the latter case the hand of art makes up for the ravages of time, and he seems many years younger.

"Few persons find themselves for the first time in the presence of General Washington, a man so renowned in the present day for his wisdom and moderation, and whose name will be transmitted with such honour to posterity, without being impressed with a certain degree of veneration and awe; nor do these emotions subside on a closer acquaintance; on the contrary, his person and deportment are such as rather tend to augment them. There is

---

1. Baker, 47–49. Henry Wansey, 1752?–1827, was a clothier from England who visited the United States—and President Washington—in 1794.

2. Ford, 8:201. Thomas Jefferson, 1743–1826, was the primary author of the Declaration of Independence and the first Secretary of State, serving under President Washington; he later served as the third president of the United States. This assessment was included in a letter to William Branch Giles.

something very austere in his countenance, and in his manners he is uncommonly reserved. I have heard some officers, that served immediately under his command during the American war, say, that they never saw him smile during all the time that they were with him. No man has ever yet been connected with him by the reciprocal and unconstrained ties of friendship; and but a few can boast even of having been on an easy and familiar footing with him.

"The height of his person is about five feet eleven; his chest is full; and his limbs, though rather slender, well shaped and muscular. His head is small, in which respect he resembles the make of a great number of his countrymen. His eyes are of a light grey color; and in proportion to the length of his face, his nose is long. Mr. Stewart, the eminent portrait painter, told me, that there are features in his face totally different from what he ever observed in that of any other human being; the sockets for the eyes, for instance, are larger than what he ever met with before, and the upper part of the nose broader. All his features, he observed, were indicative of the strongest and most ungovernable passions, and had he been born in the forests, it was his opinion that he would have been the fiercest man among the savage tribes. In this Mr. Stewart has given proof of his great discernment and intimate knowledge of the human countenance; for although General Washington has been extolled for his great moderation and calmness, during the very trying situations in which he has so often been placed, yet those who have been acquainted with him the longest and most intimately say, that he is by nature a man of a fierce and irritable disposition, but that, like Socrates, his judgment and great self-command have always made him appear a man of a different cast in the eyes of the world. He speaks with great diffidence, and sometimes hesitates for a word; but it is always to find one particularly well adapted to his meaning. His language is manly and expressive."[1]

JOHN BERNARD, 1798

"A few weeks after my location at Annapolis I met with a most pleasing adventure, no less than an encounter with General Washington, under circumstances which most fully confirmed the impression I had formed of him. I had been to pay a visit to an acquaintance on the banks of the Potomac, a few miles below Alexandria, and was returning on horseback, in the rear of an old-fashioned chaise, the driver of which was strenuously urging his steed to an accelerated pace. The beast showed singular indifference till a lash, directed with more skill than humanity, took the skin from an old wound. The sudden pang threw the poor animal on his hind-legs, and the wheel swerving upon the bank, over went the chaise, flinging out upon the road a young woman who had been its occupant. The minute before I had perceived a horseman approaching at a gentle trot, who now broke into a gallop, and we reached the scene of the disaster together. The female was our first care. She was insensible, but had sustained no material injury. My companion supported her, while I brought some water in the crown of my hat, from a spring some way off. The driver of the chaise had landed on his legs, and, having ascertained that his spouse was not dead, seemed very well satisfied with the care she was in, and set about extricating his horse. A gush of tears announced the lady's return to sensibility, and then, as her eyes opened, her tongue gradually resumed its office, and assured us that she retained at least one faculty in perfection, as she poured forth a volley of invectives on her mate.

---

1. Baker, 50–53. Isaac Weld, 1774–1856, was an Irishman who travelled extensively in America, visiting Washington in Philadelphia on the President's birthday in 1796.

"The horse was now on his legs, but the vehicle still prostrate, heavy in its frame, and laden with at least half a ton of luggage. My fellow helper set me an example of activity in relieving it of the external weight; and, when all was clear, we grasped the wheel between us and, to the peril of our spinal columns, righted the conveyance. The horse was then put in, and we lent a hand to help up the luggage. All this helping, hauling, and lifting occupied at least half an hour, under a meridian sun in the middle of July, which fairly boiled the perspiration out of our foreheads. . . .

"When all was right, and we had assisted the lady to resume her seat, he begged us to proceed with him to Alexandria and take a drop of 'something sociable.' Finding, however, that we were unsociable, he extended his hand . . . and, when we had sufficiently felt that he was grateful, drove on.

"My companion, after an exclamation at the heat, offered very courteously to dust my coat, a favor the return of which enabled me to take a deliberate survey of his person. He was a tall, erect, well-made man, evidently advanced in years, but who appeared to have retained all the vigor and elasticity resulting from a life of temperance and exercise. His dress was a blue coat buttoned to his chin, and buckskin breeches. Though, the instant he took off his hat, I could not avoid the recognition of familiar lineaments—which, indeed, I was in the habit of seeing on every sign-post and over every fireplace—still I failed to identify him, and, to my surprise, I found that I was an object of equal speculation in his eyes. A smile at length lighted them up, and he exclaimed, 'Mr. Bernard, I believe?' I bowed. 'I had the pleasure of seeing you perform last winter in Philadelphia.' . . .

"He then learned the cause of my presence in the neighborhood, and remarked, 'You must be fatigued. If you will ride up to my house, which is not a mile distant, you can prevent any ill-effects from this exertion, by a couple of hours' rest.'

"I looked round for his dwelling, and he pointed to a building which, the day before, I had spent an hour in contemplating.

'Mount Vernon!' I exclaimed; and then, drawing back, with a stare of wonder, 'have I the honor of addressing General Washington?' With a smile, whose expression of benevolence I have rarely seen equaled, he offered his hand, and replied, 'An odd sort of introduction, Mr. Bernard; but I am pleased to find you can play so active a part in private, and without a prompter.' . . . As we rode up to his house we entered freely into conversation, first, in reference to his friends at Annapolis, then respecting my own success in America and the impressions I had received of the country.

"Flattering as such inquiries were from such a source, I must confess my own reflections on what had just passed were more absorbing. Considering that nine ordinary country gentlemen out of ten, who had seen a chaise upset near their estate, would have thought it savored neither of pride nor ill-nature to ride home and send their servants to its assistance, I could not but think that I had witnessed one of the strongest evidences of a great man's claim to his reputation—the prompt, impulsive working of a heart which having made the good of mankind . . . its religion, was never so happy as in practically displaying it. On reaching the house (which, in its compact simplicity and commanding elevation, was no bad emblem of its owner's mind), we found that Mrs. Washington was indisposed; but the general ordered refreshments in a parlor whose windows took a noble range of the Potomac. . . .

"Though I have ventured to offer some remarks on his less-known contemporaries, I feel it would be an impertinence to say a word on the public merits of a man whose character has been burning as a beacon to Europe till its qualities are as well known as the names and dates of his triumphs. My retrospect of him is purely a social one, and much do I regret . . . that it is confined to a single interview. The general impression I received from his appearance fully corresponded with the description of him by the Marquis de Chatelluz, who visited America at the close of the war. 'The great characteristic of Washington,' says he, 'is the perfect union which seems to subsist between his moral and physical qualities; so that the selection of one would enable you to judge of all the rest. If you are presented with medals of Trajan or Caesar, the features will lead you to inquire the proportions of their persons; but if you should discover in a heap of ruins the leg or arm of an antique Apollo, you would not be curious about the other parts, but content yourself with the assurance that they were all conformable to those of a god.'

"Though fourteen years had elapsed since this was written, I could perceive that it was far from being the language of mere enthusiasm. Whether you surveyed his face, open yet well defined, dignified but not arrogant, thoughtful but benign; his frame, towering and muscular, but alert from its good proportion—every feature suggested a resemblance to the spirit it encased, and showed simplicity in alliance with the sublime. The impression, therefore, was that of a most perfect whole; . . . you could not but think you looked upon a wonder, and something sacred as well as wonderful—a man fashioned by the hand of Heaven, with every requisite to achieve a great work. Thus a feeling of awe and veneration stole over you.

"In conversation his face had not much variety of expression: a look of thoughtfulness was given by the compression of the mouth and the indentation of the brow. . . . Nor had his voice, so far as I could discover in our quiet talk, much change, or richness of intonation, but he always spoke with earnestness, and his eyes (glorious conductors of the light within) burned with a steady fire which no one could mistake for mere affability; they were one grand expression of the well-known line, 'I am a man, and interested in all that concerns humanity.' In our hour and a half's conversation he touched on every topic that I brought before him with an even current of good sense, if he embellished it with little wit or verbal elegance. He spoke like a man who had felt as much as he had reflected, and reflected more than he had spoken; like one who had looked upon society rather in the mass than in detail; and who regarded the happiness of America but as the first link in a series of universal victories; for his full faith in the power of those results of civil liberty which he saw all around him led him to foresee that it would, ere long, prevail in other countries, and that the social millennium of Europe would usher in the political. . . .

"As I was engaged to dine at home, I at length rose to take my leave, not without receiving from the general a very flattering request to call on him whenever I rode by. I had the pleasure of meeting him once after this in Annapolis, and I dined with him on a public occasion at Alexandria, my impressions each time improving into a higher degree of respect and admiration."[1]

Gouverneur Morris, 1799

"Born to high destinies, he was fashioned for them by the hand of nature. His form was noble—his port majestic. On his front were enthroned the virtues which exalt, and those which adorn the human character. So dignified his deportment, no man could approach him but with respect—none was great in his presence. You all have seen him, and you all have felt the reverence he inspired; it was such, that to command, seemed in him but the exercise of an ordinary function, while others felt a duty to obey, which (anterior to the injunctions of civil ordinance, or the compulsion of a military code) was imposed by the high behests of nature.

"He had every title to command—Heaven, in giving him the higher qualities of the soul, had given also the tumultuous passions which accompany greatness, and frequently tarnish its luster. With them was his first contest, and his first victory was over himself. So great the empire he had there acquired, that calm-

---

1. Bernard, 85–93. John Bernard, 1756–1828, was an English actor and biographer who met Washington by chance in 1798.

ness of manner and of conduct distinguished him through life. Yet, those who have seen him strongly moved, will bear witness that his wrath was terrible; they have seen boiling in his bosom, passion almost too mighty for man; yet, when just bursting into act, that strong passion was controlled by his stronger mind.

"Having thus a perfect command of himself, he could rely on the full exertion of his powers, in whatever direction he might order them to act. He was therefore clear, decided and unembarrassed by any consideration of himself. Such consideration did not even dare to intrude on his reflections. Hence it was, that he beheld not only the affairs that were passing around him, but those also in which he was personally engaged, with the coolness of an unconcerned spectator. They were to him as events historically recorded. His judgment was always clear, because his mind was pure. And seldom, if ever, will a sound understanding be met with in the company of a corrupt heart.

"In the strength of judgment lay, indeed, one chief excellence of his character. Leaving to feebler minds that splendor of genius, which, while it enlightens others, too often dazzles the possessor; he knew how best to use the rays which genius might emit, and carry into act its best conceptions.

"So modest, he wished not to attract attention, but observed in silence, and saw deep into the human heart. Of a thousand propositions he knew to distinguish the best; and to select among a thousand the man most fitted for his purpose. . . .

"In him were the courage of a soldier, the intrepidity of a chief, the fortitude of a hero. He had given to the impulsions of bravery all the calmness of his character, and, if in the moment of danger, his manner was distinguishable from that of common life, it was by superior ease and grace.

"To each desire he had taught the lessons of moderation. Prudence became therefore the companion of his life. Never in the public, never in the private hour, did she abandon him even for a moment. And, if in the small circle, where he might safely think

aloud, she should have slumbered amid convivial joy, his quick
sense of what was just, and decent, and fit, stood ever ready to
awaken her at the slightest alarm.

"Knowing how to appreciate the world, its gifts and glories, he
was truly wise. Wise also in selecting the objects of his pursuit.
And wise in adopting just means to compass honorable ends."[1]

ABIGAIL ADAMS, 1799

"I wrote to you the day after we received the account of the
death of General Washington. This event so important to our
country at this period, will be universally deplored. No man ever
lived, more deservedly beloved and respected. The praise and I
may say adulation which followed his administration for several
years, never made him forget that he was a man, subject to the
weakness and frailty attached to human nature. He never grew
giddy, but ever maintained a modest diffidence of his own talents,
and if that was an error, it was of the amiable and engaging kind,
though it might lead sometimes to a want of decisions in some
great emergencies. Possessed of power, possessed of an extensive
influence, he never used it but for the benefit of his country. Witness his retirement to private life when peace closed the scenes
of war; when called by the unanimous suffrages of the people
to the chief magistracy of the nation, he acquitted himself to the
satisfaction and applause of all good men. When assailed by faction, when reviled by party, he suffered with dignity, and retired
from his exalted station with a character which malice could not
wound, nor envy tarnish. If we look through the whole tenor of
his life, history will not produce to us a parallel."[2]

---

1. Baker, 73–75.
2. Mitchell, 221.

JEDIDIAH MORSE, 1799

"General Washington in his person was tall, upright, and well made; in his manners easy and unaffected. His eyes were of a bluish cast, not prominent, indicative of deep thoughtfulness, and when in action, on great occasions remarkably lively. His features strong, manly, and commanding; his temper reserved and serious; his countenance grave, composed, and sensible. There was in his whole appearance an unusual dignity and gracefulness which at once secured for him profound respect, and cordial esteem. He seemed born to command his fellow men. In his official capacity he received applicants for favors, and answered their requests with so much ease, condescension and kindness, as that each retired, believing himself a favorite of his chief. He had an excellent and well cultivated understanding; a correct, discerning, and comprehensive mind; a memory remarkably retentive; energetic passions under perfect control; a judgment sober, deliberate, and sound. He was a man of the strictest honor and honesty, fair and honorable in his dealings; and punctual to his engagements. His disposition was mild, kind, and generous. Candor, sincerity, moderation, and simplicity, were, in common, prominent features in his character; but when an occasion called, he was capable of displaying the most determined bravery, firmness, and independence. He was an affectionate husband, a faithful friend, a humane master, and a father to the poor. He lived in the unvarying habits of regularity, temperance, and industry. He steadily rose at the dawn of day, and retired to rest usually at 9 o'clock in the evening. The intermediate hours all had their proper business assigned them. In his allotments for the revolving hours, religion was not forgotten. Feeling, what he so often publicly acknowledged, his entire dependence on God, he daily, at stated seasons, retired to his closet, to worship at his footstool, and to ask his divine blessing. He was remarkable for his strict observation of the Sabbath, and exemplary in his attendance on public worship.

"Of his faith in the truth and excellence of the holy scriptures, he gave evidence, not only by his excellent and most exemplary life, but in his writings; especially when he ascribes the meliorated condition of mankind, and the increased blessings of society, 'above all, to the PURE and benign light REVELATION;' and when he offers to GOD his earnest prayer, 'that he would most graciously be pleased to dispose us all to do justice, to love mercy, and to demean ourselves with that charity, humility, and pacific temper of mind, which were the characteristics of the DIVINE AUTHOR OF OUR BLESSED RELIGION; without an humble imitation of whose example, in these things, we can never hope to be a happy nation.' In an address to him, immediately after he commenced his presidency over the United States, from a venerable and respectable body of men, who were in the best situation to know his religious character, and who, no doubt, expressed what they knew, is the following testimony to his faith in Christianity. 'But we derive a presage,' say they, 'even more flattering, from the piety of your character. Public virtue is the most certain means of public felicity; and religion is the surest basis of virtue. We therefore esteem it a peculiar happiness to behold in our chief magistrate, a steady, uniform, AVOWED friend of the Christian religion; who has commenced his administration in rational and exalted sentiments of piety, and who, in his private conduct, adorns the doctrines of the gospel of Christ.' Grounded on these pure and excellent doctrines, to which his life was so conformable; copying, as he did, with such exemplary strictness and uniformity, the precepts of Christ, we have strong consolation and joy in believing, that ere this, he has heard from his God and Savior, this enrapturing sentence, Well done good and faithful servant, enter into the joy of your Lord.

"What a blessing to the world, what an honour to human nature, is a character thus 'throughout sublime'! What a bright exemplar for kings, for princes, for rulers of every name, for warriors, for farmers, for Christians, for mankind! Thanks be to God for so rich a gift; praise to his name for bestowing it on our nation, and thus distinguishing it above all others on the globe, and let all the PEOPLE OF COLUMBIA, WITH ONE VOICE, SAY AMEN."[1]

FISHER AMES, 1800

"It is natural that the gratitude of mankind should be drawn to their benefactors. A number of these have successively arisen who were no less distinguished for the elevation of their virtues than the luster of their talents. Of those, however, who were born, and who acted through life as if they were born, not for themselves, but for their country and the whole human race, how few, alas! are recorded in the long annals of ages, and how wide the intervals of time and space that divide them. In all this dreary length of way, they appear like five or six lighthouses on as many thousand miles of coast; they gleam upon the surrounding darkness with an inextinguishable splendor, like stars seen through a mist; but they are seen, like stars, to cheer, to guide, and to save. Washington is now added to that small number. Already he attracts curiosity, like a newly discovered star, whose benignant light will travel on to the world's and time's farthest bounds. Already his name is hung up by history as conspicuously as if it sparkled in one of the constellations of the sky.

"By commemorating his death, we are called this day to yield the homage that is due to virtue; to confess the common debt of mankind as well as our own; and to pronounce for posterity, now dumb, that eulogium which they will delight to echo ten ages hence, when we are dumb. . . . Two Washingtons come not in one age. . . .

"With whatever fidelity I might execute this task, I know that some would prefer a picture drawn to the imagination. They would have our Washington represented of a giant's size and

---

1. Baker, 76–79.

in the character of a hero of romance. They who love to wonder better than to reason would not be satisfied with the contemplation of a great example, unless in the exhibition it should be so distorted into prodigy as to be both incredible and useless. Others,—I hope but few,—who think meanly of human nature, will deem it incredible that even Washington should think with as much dignity and elevation as he acted; and they will grovel in vain in the search for mean and selfish motives that could incite and sustain him to devote his life to his country. . . .

"Such a life as Washington's cannot derive honor from the circumstances of birth and education, though it throws back a luster upon both. With an inquisitive mind that always profited by the lights of others and was unclouded by passions of its own, he acquired a maturity of judgment, rare in age, unparalleled in youth. Perhaps no young man had so early laid up a life's stock of materials for solid reflection, or settled so soon the principles and habits of his conduct. Gray experience listened to his counsels with respect, and, at a time when youth is almost privileged to be rash, Virginia committed the safety of her frontier, and ultimately the safety of America, not merely to his valor,—for that would be scarcely praise,—but to his prudence. . . .

"When Washington heard the voice of his country in distress, his obedience was prompt; and though his sacrifices were great, they cost him no effort. Neither the object nor the limits of my plan permit me to dilate on the military events of the Revolutionary War. . . . When overmatched by numbers, a fugitive with a little band of faithful soldiers, the States as much exhausted as dismayed, he explored his own undaunted heart and found there resources to retrieve our affairs. We have seen him display as much valor as gives fame to heroes, and as consummate prudence as insures success to valor; fearless of dangers that were personal to him, hesitating and cautious when they affected his country; preferring fame before safety or repose, and duty before fame.

"Rome did not owe more to Fabius than America to Washington. Our nation shares with him the singular glory of having conducted a civil war with mildness and a revolution with order. . . .

"Although it was impossible that such merit as Washington's should not produce envy, it was scarcely possible that, with such a transcendent reputation, he should have rivals. Accordingly, he was unanimously chosen President of the United States.

"As a general and a patriot, the measure of his glory was already full; there was no fame left for him to excel but his own; and even that task, the mightiest of all his labors, his civil magistracy has accomplished. . . .

"Such was the state of public affairs; and did it not seem perfectly to insure uninterrupted harmony to the citizens? Did they not, in respect to their government and its administration, possess their whole heart's desire? They had seen and suffered long the want of an efficient constitution; they had freely ratified it; they saw Washington, their tried friend, the father of his country, invested with its powers; they knew that he could not exceed or betray them without forfeiting his own reputation. Consider for a moment what a reputation it was: such as no man ever before possessed by so clear a title and in so high a degree. His fame seemed in its purity to exceed even its brightness; office took honor from his acceptance, but conferred none. Ambition stood awed and darkened by his shadow. For where, through the wide earth, was the man so vain as to dispute precedence with him? or what were the honors that could make the possessor Washington's superior? Refined and complex as the ideas of virtue are, even the gross could discern in his life the infinite superiority of her rewards. Mankind perceived some change in their ideas of greatness; the splendor of power, and even the name of conqueror, had grown dim in their eyes. They did not know that Washington could augment his fame; but they knew and felt that the world's wealth, and its empire too, would be a bribe far beneath his acceptance.

"This is not exaggeration; never was confidence in a man and a chief magistrate more widely diffused or more solidly established. . . .

"How great he appeared while he administered the government, how much greater when he retired from it, . . . how his life was unspotted like his fame, and how his death was worthy of his life, are so many distinct subjects of instruction, and each of them singly more than enough for an eulogium. I leave the task, however, to history and to posterity; they will be faithful to it. . . .

"The best evidence of reputation is a man's whole life. We have now, alas! all Washington's before us. There has scarcely appeared a really great man whose character has been more admired in his lifetime, or less correctly understood by his admirers. When it is comprehended, it is no easy task to delineate its excellencies in such a manner as to give to the portrait both interest and resemblance; for it requires thought and study to understand the true ground of the superiority of his character over many others, whom he resembled in the principles of action and even in the manner of acting. But perhaps he excels all the great men that ever lived in the steadiness of his adherence to his maxims of life and in the uniformity of all his conduct to the same maxims. These maxims, though wise, were yet not so remarkable for their wisdom as for their authority over his life; for if there were any errors in his judgment—and he discovered as few as any man—we know of no blemishes in his virtue. He was the patriot without reproach; he loved his country well enough to hold his success in serving it as an ample recompense. Thus far self-love and love of country coincided; but when his country needed sacrifices that no other man could make, or perhaps would be willing to make, he did not even hesitate. This was virtue in its most exalted character. . . .

"It is, indeed, almost as difficult to draw his character as the portrait of virtue. . . . His preeminence is not so much to be seen in the display of any one virtue as in the possession of them all and in the practice of the most difficult. Hereafter, therefore, his character must be studied before it will be striking; and then it will be admitted as a model, a precious one to a free republic.

"It is not less difficult to speak of his talents.

"They were adapted to lead, without dazzling, mankind, and to draw forth and employ the talents of others, without being misled by them. In this he was certainly superior, that he neither mistook nor misapplied his own. His great modesty and reserve would have concealed them, if great occasions had not called them forth; and then, as he never spoke from the affectation to shine nor acted from any sinister motives, it is from their effects only that we are to judge of their greatness and extent. In public trusts, where men, acting conspicuously, are cautious, and in those private concerns, where few conceal or resist their weaknesses, Washington was uniformly great, pursuing right conduct from right maxims. His talents were such as assist a sound judgment and ripen with it. His prudence was consummate, and seemed to take the direction of his powers and passions; for, as a soldier, he was more solicitous to avoid mistakes that might be fatal than to perform exploits that are brilliant, and, as a statesman, to adhere to just principles, however old, than to pursue novelties; and therefore, in both characters, his qualities were singularly adapted to the interests and were tried in the greatest perils of the country. His habits of inquiry were so far remarkable that he was never satisfied with investigation nor desisted from it so long as he had less than all the light that he could obtain upon a subject, and then he made his decision without bias.

"This command over the partialities that so generally stop men short, or turn them aside, in their pursuit of truth is one of the chief causes of his unvaried course of right conduct in so many difficult scenes, where every human actor must be presumed to err. If he had strong passions, he had learned to subdue them and to be moderate and mild. If he had weaknesses, he concealed them, which is rare, and excluded them from the government of his temper and conduct, which is still more rare. If he loved fame, he never made improper compliances for what is called popularity. The fame he enjoyed is of the kind that will last forever; yet it was rather the effect than the motive of his conduct. . . . Such a citizen would do honor to any country. The constant veneration and affection of his country will show that it was worthy of such a citizen."[1]

TIMOTHY DWIGHT, 1800

"General Washington was great, not by means of that brilliancy of mind, often appropriately termed genius, and usually coveted for ourselves, and our children; and almost as usually attended with qualities, which preclude wisdom, and depreciate or forbid worth; but by a constitutional character more happily formed. His mind was in deed inventive and full of resources; but its energy appears to have been originally directed to that which is practical and useful, and not to that which is showy and specious. His judgment was clear and intuitive beyond that of most who have lived, and seemed instinctively to discern the proper answer to the celebrated Roman question: *Cui bono erit?* To this his incessant attention, and unwearied observation, which nothing, whether great or minute, escaped, doubtless contributed in a high degree. What he observed he treasured up, and thus added daily to his stock of useful knowledge. Hence, although his early education was in a degree confined, his mind became possessed of extensive, various, and exact information. Perhaps there never was a mind, on which theoretical speculations had less influence, and the decisions of common sense more.

"At the same time, no man ever more earnestly or uniformly, sought advice, or regarded it, when given, with more critical at-

---

1. Allen, 1:519–38. This description is taken from a eulogy Ames delivered two months after Washington's death.

tention. The opinion of friends and enemies, of those who abetted, and of those who opposed, his own system, he explored, and secured alike. His own opinions, also, he submitted to his proper counselors, and often to others; with a demand, that they should be sifted, and exposed, without any tenderness to them because they were his; insisting, that they should be considered as opinions merely, and, as such, should be subjected to the freest and most severe investigation.

"When any measure of importance was to be acted on, he delayed the formation of his judgment until the last moment; that he might secure to himself, always, the benefit of every hint, opinion, and circumstance, which might contribute either to confirm, or change, his decision. Hence, probably, it in a great measure arose, that he was so rarely committed; and that his decisions have so rarely produced regret; and have been so clearly justified both by their consequences and the judgment of mankind.

"With this preparation, he formed a judgment finally and wholly his own; and although no man was ever more anxious before a measure was adopted, probably no man was ever less anxious afterward. He had done his duty, and left the issue to Providence.

"To all this conduct his high independence of mind greatly contributed. By this I intend a spirit, which dares to do its duty, against friends and enemies, and in prosperous and adverse circumstances, alike; and which, when it has done its duty, is regardless of opinions and consequences.

"Nor was he less indebted to his peculiar firmness. He not only dared to act in this manner, but uniformly sustained the same tone of thought and feeling, such, as he was at the decision, he ever after continued to be; and all men despaired of operating on him unless through the medium of conviction. The same unchanging spirit supported him through every part of his astonishing trials, during the war; and exhibited him as exactly the same man after a defeat, as after a victory; neither elated nor depressed, but always grave, serene, and prepared for the event.

"From other great men he was distinguished by an exemption from favoritism. No man ever so engrossed his attachment, as to be safe, for a moment, from deserved reproof, or censure; nor was any man ever so disrelished by him, as, on that account, to fail of receiving from him whatever applause, or services his merit could claim. Hence his friends feared, and his enemies respected him.

"His moderation and self-government were such that he was always in his own power, and never in the power of any other person. Whatever passions he felt, they rarely appeared. His conduct, opinions, and life, wore unusually the character of mere intellect. Hence he was never found unguarded, or embarrassed; but was always at full liberty to do that, and that only, which expediency and duty demanded. A striking instance of this trait in his character is seen in the well-known fact; that he never exculpated himself from any charge, nor replied to any calumny. His accusers, for such he had, had opportunity to make the most of their accusations; his calumniators, if their consciences permitted, to sleep in peace.

"His justice was exact, but tempered with the utmost humanity, which the occasion would suffer. His truth no sober man, who knew him, probably ever doubted. Watchful against his own exposures to error, he was rarely found erring; jealous of doing injustice, if he has done injustice, it is yet, I believe, unrecorded.

"His reservedness has been at times censured. To me it appears to have been an important and necessary characteristic of a person situated as he was. In familiar life a communicative disposition is generally pleasing, and often useful; in his high stations it would have been dangerous. One unguarded or ambiguous expression might have produced evils, the remedy of which would have been beyond even his own power. No such expression is recorded of him.

"His punctuality was extreme. He rose always with the dawn; he dined at a given minute; he attended every appointment at the moment. Hence his business public and private was always done at the proper time, and always beforehand.

"No person appears to have had a higher sense of decorum, and universal propriety. The eye, following his public and private life, traces an unexceptionable propriety, an exact decorum, in every action; in every word; in his demeanor to men of every class; in his public communications; in his convivial entertainments; in his letters; and in his familiar conversation; from which bluntness, flattery, witticism, indelicacy, negligence, passion, and overaction, were alike excluded.

"From these things happily combined, always seen, and seen always in their native light, without art, or affectation, it arose, that, wherever he appeared, an instinctive awe and veneration attended him on the part of all men. Every man, however great in his own opinion, or in reality, shrunk in his presence, and became conscious of an inferiority, which he never felt before. Whilst he encouraged every man, particularly every stranger, and peculiarly every diffident man, and raised him to self-possession, no sober person, however secure he might think himself of his esteem, ever presumed to draw too near him.

"With respect to his religious character there have been different opinions. No one will be surprised at this, who reflects, that this is a subject, about which, in all circumstances not involving inspired testimony, doubts may and will exist. The evidence concerning it must of course arise from an induction of particulars. Some will induce more of these particulars, and others fewer; some will rest on one class, or collection, others on another; and some will give more, and others less, weight to those which are induced; according to their several modes, and standards, of judging. The question in this, and all other cases, must be finally determined before another tribunal, than that of human judgment; and to that tribunal it must ultimately be left. For my own part, I have considered his numerous and uniform public and most solemn declarations of his high veneration for religion, his exemplary and edifying attention to public worship, and his constancy in secret devotion, as proofs, sufficient to satisfy every person, willing to be satisfied. I shall only add, that if he was not a Christian, he was more like one, than any man of the same description, whose life has been hitherto recorded.

"As a warrior, his merit has, I believe, been fully and readily acknowledged; yet I have doubted whether it has always been justly estimated. His military greatness lay not principally in desperate sallies of courage; in the daring and brilliant exploits of a partisan: These would have ill suited his station, and most probably have ruined his cause and country. It consisted in the formation of extensive and masterly plans; effectual preparations, the cautious prevention of great evils, and the watchful seizure of every advantage; in combining heterogeneous materials into one military body, producing a system of military and political measures, concentering universal confidence, and diffusing an influence next to magical; in comprehending a great scheme of war, pursuing a regular system of acquiring strength for his country, and wearing out the strength of his enemies. To his conduct, both military and political, may, with exact propriety, be applied the observation, which has been often made concerning his courage; that in the most hazardous situations no man ever saw his countenance change."[1]

---

1. Baker, 110–15. Timothy Dwight, 1752–1817, was an army chaplain during the Revolutionary War; he served as president of Yale College from 1795 until his death. This quotation is an extract from a eulogy Dwight gave two months after Washington's death.

ALEXANDER HAMILTON, 1800

"Very different from the practice of Mr. Adams was that of the modest and sage Washington. He consulted much, pondered much, resolved slowly, resolved surely."[1]

JOHN MARSHALL, 1807

"General Washington was rather above the common size, his frame was robust, and his constitution vigorous, capable of enduring great fatigue, and requiring a considerable degree of exercise for the preservation of his health. His exterior created in the beholder the idea of strength united with manly gracefulness.

"His manners were rather reserved than free, though they partook nothing of that dryness and sternness which accompany reserve when carried to an extreme; and on all proper occasions, he could relax sufficiently to show how highly he was gratified by the charms of conversation, and the pleasures of society. His person and whole deportment exhibited an unaffected and indescribable dignity, unmingled with haughtiness, of which all who approached him were sensible; and the attachment of those who possessed his friendship and enjoyed his intimacy, was ardent but always respectful.

"His temper was humane, benevolent, and conciliatory; but there was a quickness in his sensibility to anything apparently offensive, which experience had taught him to watch and to correct.

"In the management of his private affairs he exhibited an exact yet liberal economy. His funds were not prodigally wasted on capricious and ill examined schemes, nor refused to beneficial though costly improvements. They remained therefore compe-

---

1. Syrett, 12:214. Alexander Hamilton, 1755 or 1757–1804, served as senior aide-de-camp to Washington during the Revolutionary War, as a delegate to the Constitutional Convention, and as first Secretary of the Treasury.

tent to that expensive establishment which his reputation, added to a hospitable temper, had in some measure imposed upon him; and to those donations which real distress has a right to claim from opulence.

"He made no pretensions to that vivacity which fascinates, or to that wit which dazzles and frequently imposes on the understanding. More solid than brilliant, judgment rather than genius constituted the most prominent feature of his character.

"As a military man, he was brave, enterprising, and cautious. That malignity which has sought to strip him of all the higher qualities of a general, has conceded to him personal courage, and a firmness of resolution which neither dangers nor difficulties could shake. But candor will allow him other great and valuable endowments. If his military course does not abound with splendid achievements, it exhibits a series of judicious measures adapted to circumstances, which probably saved his country. . . .

"Possessing an energetic and distinguishing mind, on which the lessons of experience were never lost, his errors, if he committed any, were quickly repaired; and those measures which the state of things rendered most advisable were seldom if ever neglected. Inferior to his adversary in the numbers, in the equipment, and in the discipline of his troops, it is evidence of real merit that no great and decisive advantages were ever obtained over him, and that the opportunity to strike an important blow never passed away unused. . . .

"In his civil administration, as in his military career, were exhibited ample and repeated proofs of that practical good sense, of that sound judgment which is perhaps the most rare, and is certainly the most valuable quality of the human mind. Devoting himself to the duties of his station, and pursuing no object distinct from the public good, he was accustomed to contemplate at a distance those critical situations in which the United States might probably be placed; and to digest, before the occasion required action, the line of conduct which it would be proper to observe. Taught to distrust first impressions, he sought to acquire all the information which was obtainable, and to hear, without prejudice, all the reasons which could be urged for or against a particular measure. His own judgment was suspended until it became necessary to determine, and his decisions, thus maturely made, were seldom if ever to be shaken. His conduct therefore was systematic, and the great objects of his administration were steadily pursued.

"Respecting, as the first magistrate in a free government must ever do, the real and deliberate sentiments of the people, their gusts of passion passed over without ruffling the smooth surface of his mind.

"Trusting to the reflecting good sense of the nation for approbation and support, he had the magnanimity to pursue its real interests, in opposition to its temporary prejudices; and, though far from being regardless of popular favor, he could never stoop to retain, by deserving to lose it. In more instances than one, we find him committing his whole popularity to hazard, and pursuing steadily, in opposition to a torrent which would have overwhelmed a man of ordinary firmness, that course which had been dictated by a sense of duty.

"In speculation, he was a real republican, devoted to the constitution of his country, and to that system of equal political rights on which it is founded. But between a balanced republic and a democracy, the difference is like that between order and chaos. Real liberty, he thought, was to be preserved, only by preserving the authority of the laws, and maintaining the energy of government. Scarcely did society present two characters which, in his opinion, less resembled each other, than a patriot and a demagogue.

"No man has ever appeared upon the theatre of public action, whose integrity was more incorruptible, or whose principles were more perfectly free from the contamination of those selfish and unworthy passions, which find their nourishment in the conflicts of party. Having no views which required concealment, his real and avowed motives were the same; and his whole correspondence does not furnish a single case, from which even an enemy would infer that he was capable, under any circumstances, of stooping to the employment of duplicity. No truth can be uttered with more confidence than that his ends were always upright, and his means always pure. He exhibits the rare example of a politician to whom wiles were absolutely unknown, and whose professions to foreign governments, and to his own countrymen, were always sincere. In him was fully exemplified the real distinction, which forever exists, between wisdom and cunning, and the importance as well as truth of the maxim that 'honesty is the best policy.'

"If Washington possessed ambition, that passion was, in his bosom, so regulated by principles, or controlled by circumstances, that it was neither vicious nor turbulent. Intrigue was never employed as the means of its gratification, nor was personal aggrandizement its object. The various high and important stations to which he was called by the public voice were unsought by himself; and in consenting to fill them, he seems rather to have yielded to a general conviction that the interests of his country would be thereby promoted, than to his particular inclination.

"Neither the extraordinary partiality of the American people, the extravagant praises which were bestowed upon him, nor the inveterate opposition and malignant calumnies which he experienced, had any visible influence upon his conduct. The cause is to be looked for in the texture of his mind.

"In him, that innate and unassuming modesty which adulation would have offended, which the voluntary plaudits of millions could not betray into indiscretion, and which never obtruded upon others his claims to superior consideration, was happily blended with a high and correct sense of personal dignity, and with a just consciousness of that respect which is due to station. Without exertion, he could maintain the happy medium between that arrogance which wounds, and that facility which allows the office to be degraded in the person who fills it.

"It is impossible to contemplate the great events which have occurred in the United States under the auspices of Washington, without ascribing them, in some measure, to him. If we ask the causes of the prosperous issue of a war, against the successful termination of which there were so many probabilities? of the good which was produced, and the ill which was avoided during an administration fated to contend with the strongest prejudices that a combination of circumstances and of passions could produce? of the constant favor of the great mass of his fellow citizens, and of the confidence which, to the last moment of his life, they reposed in him? the answer, so far as these causes may be found in his character, will furnish a lesson well meriting the attention of those who are candidates for political fame.

"Endowed by nature with a sound judgment, and an accurate discriminating mind, he feared not that laborious attention which made him perfectly master of those subjects, in all their relations, on which he was to decide: and this essential quality was guided by an unvarying sense of moral right, which would tolerate the employment only of those means that would bear the most rigid examination; by a fairness of intention which neither sought nor required disguise: and by a purity of virtue which was not only untainted, but unsuspected."[1]

Gouverneur Morris, 1807

"In approving highly your character of Washington [as drawn in Marshall's biography], permit me to add that few men of such steady, persevering industry ever existed, and perhaps no one

---

1. Baker, 142–48. John Marshall, 1755–1835, was an officer in the Revolutionary War; he served as chief justice of the United States from 1801 until his death. He published a five-volume biography of Washington between 1804 and 1807, which included the extract given here.

who so completely commanded himself. Thousands have learned
to restrain their passions, though few among them had to contend with passions so violent. But the self-command to which I
allude was of higher grade. He could, at the dictate of reason,
control his will and command himself to act. Others may have
acquired a portion of the same authority; but who could, like
Washington, at any moment command the energies of his mind
to a cheerful exertion?"[1]

JOHN JAY, 1811

"His administration raised the nation out of confusion into order, out of degradation and distress into reputation and prosperity. It found us withering—it left us flourishing."[2]

THOMAS JEFFERSON, 1814

"I think I knew General Washington intimately and thoroughly; and were I called on to delineate his character, it should
be in terms like these.

"His mind was great and powerful, without being of the very
first order; his penetration strong, though not so acute as that of
a Newton, Bacon or Locke; and, as far as he saw, no judgment
was ever sounder. It was slow in operation, being little aided by
invention or imagination, but sure in conclusion. . . . He was
incapable of fear, meeting personal dangers with the calmest un-
concern. Perhaps the strongest feature in his character was prudence, never acting until every circumstance, every consideration,
was maturely weighed; refraining, if he saw a doubt, but, when,
once decided, going through with his purpose whatever obsta-

---

1. Morris, 2:492. This description was included in a letter to John Marshall.
2. Jay, 2:341.

cles opposed. His integrity was most pure, his justice the most inflexible I have ever known, no motives of interest or consanguinity, of friendship or hatred, being able to bias his decision. He was, indeed, in every sense of the words, a wise, a good, and a great man. His temper was naturally irritable and high-toned; but reflection and resolution had obtained a firm and habitual ascendency over it. If ever, however, it broke its bonds, he was most tremendous in his wrath.

"In his expenses he was honorable, but exact; liberal in contributions to whatever promised utility; but frowning and unyielding on all visionary projects, and all unworthy calls on his charity. His heart was not warm in its affections; but he exactly calculated every man's value, and gave him a solid esteem proportioned to it. His person, you know, was fine, his stature exactly what one would wish, his deportment easy, erect and noble; the best horseman of his age, and the most graceful figure that could be seen on horseback. Although in the circle of his friends, where he might be unreserved with safety, he took a free share in conversation, his colloquial talents were not above mediocrity, possessing neither copiousness of ideas, nor fluency of words.

"In public when called on for a sudden opinion, he was unready, short and embarrassed. Yet he wrote readily, rather diffusely, in an easy and correct style. This he had acquired by conversation with the world, for his education was merely reading, writing and common arithmetic, to which he added surveying at a later day. His time was employed in action chiefly, reading little, and that only in agriculture and English history. His correspondence became necessarily extensive, and, with journalizing his agricultural proceedings, occupied most of his leisure hours within doors. On the whole, his character was, in its mass, perfect, in nothing bad, in few points indifferent; and it may be truly said, that never did nature and fortune combine more perfectly to make a man great, and to place him in the same constellation with whatever worthies have merited from man an everlasting remembrance. For his was the singular destiny and merit, of leading the armies of his country successfully through an arduous war, for the establishment of its independence; of conducting its councils through the birth of a government, new in its forms and principles, until it had settled down into a quiet and orderly train; and of scrupulously obeying the laws through the whole of his career, civil and military, of which the history of the world furnishes no other example.

" . . . The soundness of [his judgment] gave him correct views of the rights of man, and his severe justice devoted him to them. He has often declared to me that he considered our new constitution as an experiment on the practicability of republican government, and with what dose of liberty man could be trusted for his own good; that he was determined the experiment should have a fair trial, and would lose the last drop of his blood in support of it.

" . . . I felt on his death, with my countrymen, that 'verily a great man hath fallen this day in Israel.'"[1]

---

1. Ford, 11:448–51.

Sources

Abbot, W. W., et al., eds., *The Papers of George Washington*, Presidential Series. 16 vols. Charlottesville and London: University Press of Virginia, 1987–2011.

Adams, Abigail. *Letters of Mrs. Adams: The Wife of John Adams.* 2d ed. 2 vols. Boston: Charles Little and James Brown, 1940.

Adams, Charles Francis, ed. *The Works of John Adams: Second President of the United States.* 10 vols. Boston: Little, Brown and Co., 1851, 1853.

Allen, William B., ed. *Works of Fisher Ames.* 2 vols. Indianapolis: Liberty Classics, 1983.

Ames, Seth, ed. *Works of Fisher Ames.* 2 vols. Boston: Little, Brown and Co., 1854.

Baker, W. S. *Character Portraits of Washington.* Philadelphia: Robert M. Lindsay, 1887.

Bancroft, George. *History of the United States of America, from the Discovery of the Continent.* New York: D. Appleton and Co., 1885.

Bernard, John. *Retrospections of America, 1797–1811.* New York: Harper & Brothers, 1887.

Book of Common Prayer, 1751. In Peter A. Lillback and Jerry Newcombe. *George Washington's Sacred Fire.* King of Prussia, PA.: Providence Forum Press, 2006.

Burnett, Edmund C., ed. *Letters of Members of the Continental Congress.* 7 vols. Washington, D.C.: Carnegie Institution of Washington, 1921–36.

Butterfield, Lyman H., ed. *Letters of Benjamin Rush, 1783–1813.* 2 vols. Princeton, N.J.: Princeton University Press, 1951.

Clary, David A. *Adopted Son: Washington, Lafayette, and the Friendship That Saved the Revolution.* New York: Bantam Dell, 2007.

Custis, George Washington Parke. *Recollections and Private Memoirs of Washington.* New York: Derby and Jackson, 1860.

Documentary History of the Constitution of the United States of America, 1786–1870. 3 vols. Washington, D.C.: Department of State, 1905.

Farrand, Max, ed. *Records of the Federal Convention of 1787.* 3 vols. New Haven: Yale University Press, 1911.

Federer, William J. *America's God and Country: Encyclopedia of Quotations.* St. Louis: Amerisearch, 2000.

Fitzpatrick, John C., ed. *Writings of George Washington.* 39 vols. Washington, D.C.: U.S. Government Printing Office, 1931–44.

Ford, Paul Leicester, ed. *The Works of Thomas Jefferson.* 10 vols. New York: G. P. Putnam's Sons, 1904–5.

George Washington's Rules of Civility & Decent Behavior in Company and Conversation. Mount Vernon: Mount Vernon Ladies Association, 1989.

Hamilton, Alexander, James Madison, and John Jay. *The Federalist Papers.* New York: New American Library, 1961.

Hamilton, John C., ed. *The Works of Alexander Hamilton.* 7 vols. New York: J. F. Trow, 1850.

Hatch, Louis Clinton. *The Administration of the American Revolutionary Army.* New York: Longmans, Green, and Co., 1904.

Hunter, John. "An Account of a Visit to Washington at Mount Vernon, by an English Gentleman, in 1785," *The Pennsylvania Magazine of History and Biography* 17:76–82.

Jay, William, ed. *The Life of John Jay, with Selections from His Correspondence.* New York: J. and J. Harper, 1833.

Jensen, Merrill, et al., eds. *The Documentary History of the First Federal Elections, 1788–1790.* 4 vols. Madison, WI: University of Wisconsin Press, 1976–89.

Johnson, William J. *George Washington, the Christian.* New York: Abingdon Press, 1919.

Johnston, Henry P., ed. *The Correspondence and Public Papers of John Jay.* 4 vols. New York: G.P. Putnam's Sons, 1781.

Kaminski, John P. *Founders on the Founders: Word Portraits from the American Revolutionary Era.* Charlottesville: University of Virginia Press, 2008.

Kent, William. *Memoirs and Letters of James Kent.* Boston: Little, Brown and Co., 1898.

Lucas, Stephen. *The Quotable George Washington.* Madison, WI: Madison House Publishers, 1999.

McCullough, David. *John Adams.* New York: Simon and Schuster, 2001.

Mitchell, Stewart, ed. *The New Letters of Abigail Adams, 1788–1801.* Boston: Houghton-Mifflin, 1947.

Morris, Anne Cary, ed. *The Diary and Letters of Gouverneur Morris.* 2 vols. New York: Charles Scribner's Sons, 1888.

Niles, Hezekiah. *Principles and Acts of the Revolution in America.* Baltimore, 1822.

Pennsylvania Journal and Weekly Advertiser, Nov. 14, 1787.

Quincy, Josiah. *The Journals of Major Samuel Shaw.* Boston: Wm. Crosby and H. P. Nichols, 1847.

Records of the Columbia Historical Society. Washington, D. C.: Columbia Historical Society, 1895.

Ryerson, Richard Alan, ed. *Papers of John Adams: May 1775–January 1776*. The Adams Papers. Cambridge, MA: Harvard University Press, 1979.

Schroeder, John Frederick. *Life and Times of Washington*. Albany, N.Y.: M. M. Belcher Publishing, 1903.

Schultz D., et al., eds. *Encyclopedia of Religion in American Politics*. Phoenix: Oryx Press, 1999.

Smith, Ellen Hart. *Charles Carroll of Carrollton*. New York: Russell & Russell, 1971.

Sparks, Jared, ed. *The Writings of George Washington*. 12 vols. Boston: American Stationer's Co., 1834–37.

Syrett, Howard C., ed. *The Papers of Alexander Hamilton*. 27 vols. New York: Columbia University Press, 1961–81.

Tower, Charlemagne. *The Marquis de La Fayette in the American Revolution*. 2d ed. Philadelphia: J. B. Lippincott, 1901.

Whitney, Janet. *Abigail Adams*. Boston: Little, Brown and Co., 1949.

About the Author

Jay A. Parry is a professional writer who lives in Salt Lake City, Utah. He has written, coauthored, or compiled more than two dozen published books, along with dozens of magazine articles. Some of his works include *The Real George Washington: The True Story of America's Most Indispensable Man*; *Soldiers, Statesmen, and Heroes: America's Founding Presidents*; and *U.S.I.Q.: A Constitutional Quiz Game*.

www.ingramcontent.com/pod-product-compliance
Lightning Source LLC
Chambersburg PA
CBHW031834090426
42741CB00005B/239